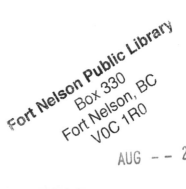

Love Is All You Need

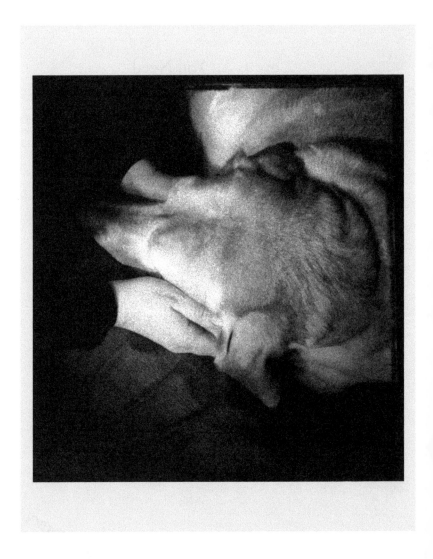

LOVE
Is All You Need

*The Revolutionary Bond-Based Approach
to Educating Your Dog*

JENNIFER
ARNOLD

SPIEGEL & GRAU • NEW YORK

Published in the United States by Spiegel & Grau, an imprint of Random House, a division of Penguin Random House LLC, New York.

SPIEGEL & GRAU and the HOUSE colophon are registered trademarks of Penguin Random House LLC.

Library of Congress Cataloging-in-Publication Data
Names: Arnold, Jennifer, author.
Title: Love is all you need : the revolutionary bond-based approach to educating your dog / Jennifer Arnold.
Description: New York : Spiegel & Grau, 2016.
Identifiers: LCCN 2015035722| ISBN 9780812996173 |
ISBN 9780812996180 (ebook)
Subjects: LCSH: Dogs—Behavior. | Dogs—Psychology. |
Human-animal relationships.
Classification: LCC SF433 .A737 2016 | DDC 636.7—dc23 LC record available at
http://lccn.loc.gov/2015035722

Printed in the United States of America on acid-free paper

randomhousebooks.com
spiegelandgrau.com

2 4 6 8 9 7 5 3 1

First Edition

Book design by Susan Turner

*To the dogs
with love and admiration*

Julia Roberts

Animals have always been a part of my life—we have had many different kinds and sizes of cats, hamsters, horses, rats, fish—but my heart has always been with dogs. When I was a little girl, I wanted to be a veterinarian. I joined the 4-H club and was on my way to my destiny. *Could there be any better job in the world,* my twelve-year-old self thought, *than playing with animals all day?* Seeing Rex Harrison talking to the animals in the movie *Doctor Dolittle* furthered my fantasy. I thought, *I have that power. I speak their language. I can ask them what's wrong, they'll tell me. I will be a great vet!*

However, as middle school became high school and science class turned into advanced biology, I saw my beautiful career as a vet come screeching to a halt. There was more practical science required than I ever realized, and I found happiness in a different career, which has luckily provided me time with lots of incredible animals over the years—horses, reptiles, monkeys, cats, and dogs. And dogs still are the winner with me. Especially my lab Louie, who was a wedding gift from my husband.

Several years ago, my husband was working on a documentary about Canine Assistants, a nonprofit based outside of Atlanta, not far from where I grew up, that raises and provides service dogs—free of charge—for people with disabilities. He met Jennifer Arnold, the founder of the organization, and got to spend time with some of the dogs, from tiny little pups to two-year-old service-dogs-in-training ready to graduate into their working lives. He knew I would be completely enchanted by the rolling green hills and red barns of this picture-perfect Georgia farm and the photogenic goldens and labs and doodle mixes romping for the camera. Of course, the centerpiece for this incredible place is the incredible Jennifer and her way with these special dogs.

Not long ago, we went back to Georgia, and one day we took a drive there as a family to visit and spent hours with the dogs. A sunny day with three kids and a seemingly endless parade of puppies—what could be better!

Jennifer is a real Doctor Dolittle. She has an uncanny ability to see the world through a dog's eyes—to experience sights, smells, sounds, and signals just as a dog does, and she allows those insights to direct her work. She, unlike me, is at home with the science, and it reinforces her brilliant intuition and understanding of what goes on in the hearts and minds of dogs. Her approach is remarkable, and her story of how dogs have truly been the compass of her life is a lovely one for all animal lovers. But maybe to all of us dog lovers, it means even more.

Contents

A Bond Beyond Measure

I love dogs. Practically from the time I could speak, dogs have always consumed a large part of my heart and mind. I actually learned my phone number as a four-year-old so that I could call home from nursery school to be certain my dogs were safe. We had a tiny Chihuahua that my brother named Dodo and a miniature poodle named Gigi. While I loved Dodo, I worshipped that small poodle. Her care and well-being were my constant concerns. And what a patient creature she was to have endured my clumsy, little-girl attempts at painting her nails and styling her hair and dressing her in some ridiculous getups.

Though I may have failed on a few of Gigi's hairdos, my desire to tend to her needs was sincere. I've always adored animals, beginning with Gigi, and felt a need to advocate for their well-being. My father, an ophthalmologist, once had to beg me to stop leaving petitions for various animal welfare causes in his office next to the patient sign-in sheet, as his visually impaired patients were confusing the forms. After the petition setback, I decided to focus my efforts more locally. In sixth grade, aided by a wonderful teacher, I organized a fundraiser for our local humane society. I wanted to encourage people to make life better for dogs. But as it turned out, that pursuit would be delayed for many years. My journey would first require that I ask dogs to help make life better for people.

It started one morning when I was sixteen years old and awoke to discover that my legs no longer worked. I remember trying to walk to the bathroom only to find that I kept falling; I was unable to stand. The diagnosis turned out to be multiple sclerosis, and the prognosis, at that time, was grim. I was told that I would likely need a wheelchair for the rest of my life. I was devastated.

My father had recently read an article in a magazine about a woman in California named Bonnie Bergin who was training dogs to help people who used wheelchairs. He knew a service dog would provide me with emotional comfort as well as physical assistance, and he reached out to Bonnie. Unfortunately, her business was new and not yet prepared to send a dog across the country for placement in Georgia. My father was deterred only briefly before recognizing that this might provide even greater incentive for me — a reason for living, a purpose.

One night, Dad sat on the edge of my bed and told me about Bonnie's program. My disappointment upon hearing that I wouldn't be able to get a dog from her quickly turned into excitement as Dad outlined his idea of starting a service-dog school of our own. We began making plans.

But things did not turn out as we'd hoped. Two weeks after his first meeting with a CPA to begin the process of obtaining nonprofit status from the IRS, my father was hit by a drunk driver on a motorcycle as he walked along a golf course near our house. Dad was badly injured. He spent that night fighting for his life at the hospital where he'd worked for most of his career. I was a true daddy's girl and he was my best friend. We spent the night in the ICU waiting room anxious for news, desperate for any sign of hope.

I knew realistically that he couldn't survive. Early the next morning, he succumbed to the massive trauma his body had endured. The doctors explained that it was easier to name the bones in his body that had *not* been broken than those that had. In the span of ten hours, I went from pleading with God to raging against him. In the end, I decided that the only reason to live when life hurt so very badly was if so doing could help other people who were suffering.

Dad was prophetic when he said that Canine Assistants would give purpose to my life, though he couldn't have imagined the circumstances that made it so. Money was extremely tight after Dad died, and it took my mom and me almost eleven years to raise the money to start Canine Assistants, but we finally succeeded in December of 1991.

Some two decades later, the amazing things I have seen dogs do for the people they love have left me in awe of their willingness and capabilities. From encouraging a six-year-old boy to say his first word, to predicting seizures some twenty minutes before they happen, to pulling a semiconscious man out of a burning house, the dogs I work with have done truly heroic things.

When I started Canine Assistants, it was with the goal of improving the lives of people in need. Fairly quickly, I realized that our dogs have that part covered—they do it naturally. Today, my job is to determine how to make it easier for dogs to be successful with their people. And I'm lucky. Every day, I have perfect opportunities to research how best to do this, since I live on the Canine Assistants property and run a program that has 110 to 140 dogs between birth and two years of age at any given time.

After twenty-five years of directing Canine Assistants, I had an epiphany about the way we relate to our dogs, which has led me to overturn many of my own methods and to question a lot of the prevailing wisdom in the dog world. The trainer who worked with us at the start of Canine Assistants was a wonderful woman, but unfortunately she was deeply steeped in the predominant training methods of the day, which included the use of pinch collars, choke chains, and ample amounts of punishment to compel dogs to do what we want them to do. While these techniques always made me uncomfortable, it took years of experience before I was confident enough to challenge the status quo. Deep down, I believe that it is essential to understand what dogs are thinking and feeling, even as we seek to control what they are doing—something that many dog trainers have traditionally discouraged as unknowable and irrelevant. I wrote about this in my first two books, *Through a Dog's Eyes* and *In a Dog's Heart.* Fortunately, there are scientists who have been working for the past two decades to prove my beliefs valid.

Among the first of these scientists were Vilmos Csányi, Adam Miklosi, and Jozsef Topal, in the Department of Ethology at Eötvös Loránd University in Budapest. Established in 1994, their research center, now known as the Family Dog Project, became the first in the scientific world dedicated to the study of the domestic dog. Before the Family Dog Project, most scientists had dismissed dogs as unworthy of serious study, believing their behavior was "contaminated" by the interference of humans.

The willingness of these scientists to brave intense criticism emboldened others interested in canine cognition and related fields to follow suit. Today, dogs are the primary focus in numerous animal research centers in prestigious institutions such as Yale University, Duke University, and the Max Planck Institute. What we know about dogs is increasing on an almost weekly basis. It is a fantastic point in history for those of us who love dogs. The data emerging from these research centers is not only fascinating, it's relevant to the way we work and live with our canine best friends. When I first met Adam Miklosi, he told me that the goal of the Family Dog Project was to publish their findings from work with dogs in the lab so that others could put them to use in the world in practical ways.

I had become increasingly aware that our current relationship with dogs is far from optimal, and the findings of these scientists produced a series of "aha moments" for me. My thinking about dogs has now evolved far beyond what I've written in my earlier books. It began with the evidence that dogs view their most beloved humans much as young toddlers view their primary parents. Functional MRIs (fMRIs) of dogs indicate that the pleasure centers in dogs' brains light up when they so much as smell beloved humans. Scientific studies have also shown that dogs, like people, are highly social, and consequently much of what they do is dictated by group expectations and codes of conduct. Dogs want to be part of our group, and they are willing to follow the lead of humans—particularly those to whom they are securely attached. Time and again, the new science backed up what my heart was telling me—that it is more important to bond with our dogs and to gain their trust than it is to overtly direct or "train" them. In fact, training in its traditional sense can actually be counterproductive, which I'll explain later.

Additionally, science has shown that dogs are capable of fairly complex cognition, far more than we ask from them routinely. For example, we've learned that dogs can reason by exclusion. So if you lay three toys on the ground in front of your dog, two that are familiar and that your dog knows by name, and one that is new, your dog can deduce that the new name goes with the new toy. Data also clearly indicates that dogs are capable of imitation and other forms of learning that go far beyond mere conditioning. These findings have led me to conclude that dogs can actually be taught to direct their own behavior and to trust in their own ability to do so. And in step with this ability to self-direct, I also believe it's important for our dogs to have confidence, and to feel that they have some measure of control over their lives, a necessary component of well-being for all animals.

At the heart of everything I learned was *the bond*, the connection which allows dogs to trust in us, while also learning to trust in themselves. It is the bond that enables what my trainer friend Allison calls the "roots and wings" effect; we make certain that our dogs are rooted in their secure bond to us, while giving them the freedom to learn and explore.

In the past, the final examination that our Canine Assistants service-dog teams had to pass in order to graduate focused on task performance on command. However, after several years of tracking the data, we realized that responsiveness to commands did not correlate to the long-term success of the teams. (Success is measured in terms of the contentment of both partners with the relationship and in terms of the human partner's improved functionality in activities of daily living because of the dog's presence.) As a matter of fact, there seemed to be something of an inverse relationship between dogs who displayed remarkable obedience and the ultimate success of the partnership. Often, the most obedient dogs appeared insecure, anxious, and generally unhappy when not being cued or directed by their human partners. The primary reason for this apparent contradiction is that in those cases, the bond had been sacrificed to the perceived need to enforce obedience.

So what does predict success for our teams? Principally, it's how much the dog and person like each other—in other words, the bond. There is a perfect correlation between a strong bond and a successful partnership. Now our practical final for the graduating teams is all about the bond. We've seen vastly improved scores on our bond scale using Bond-Based Choice Teaching®. As it happens, we now routinely have teams whose bond scores are so high that we run out of room on the chart. We've nicknamed that level of remarkable connection a *bond beyond measure*. And the teams who score in the *bond-beyond-measure* range inevitably succeed. The relationship between man and dog is unique and yet incredibly simple. It's about a bond between two entirely different species based on the most powerful of all emotions—love.

Not only did those dogs who were securely bonded to their partners behave exceedingly well, they were able to learn new things at an astonishing rate. Seeing the amazing impact of the bond on the graduating dogs, I decided to ask our staff and volunteers to stop focusing on training the dogs to perform behaviors on cue and start focusing on developing a strong relationship with the dogs. The results of this approach, which I call "Non-Training at Its Best," were extraordinary. Guiding dogs from within a secure relationship, rather than training them, produces confident, happy dogs who willingly figure out what they need to do . . . without cues or commands. It has become decidedly evident that the bond is all-important.

My exploration of how we can best establish and maintain a healthy bond with our dogs has led me to develop an entirely new approach to living and working with dogs. This isn't just a different methodology, technique, or a subtle change to an existing system—this is an entirely new philosophy about life with dogs. And it works just as well with pet dogs as it does with service dogs.

In this book, I'll explain why and how I developed my approach, Bond-Based Choice Teaching, and exactly how you can use it with your own dog, no matter if your dog is a puppy, a teen, or a mature adult. I'll also share the latest research and information about dogs and specific techniques for working with them. It is my hope that this information will make it easier for you and your dog to have a great relationship. But in the end, knowledge and skill aren't what matters most. Love is!

Love Is All You Need

One

Troubled by Training

We obviously care deeply about our dogs, yet it has become clear that we may not be acting in their best interest. Today, dogs suffer from stress-based disorders such as phobias, anxieties, hyperactivity, and obsessive-compulsive behavior at an unprecedented rate. Dr. Kenneth Martin, a veterinary behaviorist in Texas, concludes from recent data that behavior problems are the number one reason that pets are taken to shelters or euthanized. Survey research conducted on behalf of the makers of Thundershirt, a swaddling garment designed to reduce anxiety in dogs, indicated that dog owners spend over $1 billion annually dealing with their dogs' stress-related behaviors. I believe that traditional methods of training are in large part to blame for this epidemic. If we are to help our dogs, we need a new approach to living and working with them that moves beyond *training*. It's time for a shift in the paradigm.

Of course, there are times that stress and fear can actually be helpful, acting as warning signals and encouraging us to take needed action. Being hungry is stressful, but as long as there is access to food, the stress is constructive, encouraging the intake of essential nutrients. Similarly, when a potential predator suddenly appears, fear promotes the immediate search for safety. However, when food is not readily available, the stress of hunger can become damaging, causing anxiety and feelings of desperation. Likewise, when a potential predator approaches a dog who is confined to a crate and unable to escape, the fear can again be damaging, both mentally and physically.

In fact, a study conducted by Dr. Nancy Dreschel, a veterinarian at Pennsylvania State University, showed that dogs who were significantly fearful of strangers died approximately six months earlier than their peers. The results of other studies, too numerous for detailed review, indicate that living with chronic stress and anxiety is harmful in a myriad of ways, from increased blood pressure to decreased bone density. We know that a state of constant fear is not a healthy, happy place to live, yet many of our dogs appear to have taken up residency there.

Why our dogs are so stressed is a question with multiple complex answers. First, we have put them in an environment that makes it impossible for them to alleviate their own stress and anxiety. When it was common and acceptable for dogs to run loose, they could hunt for their own food and determine ways to keep themselves safe from harm. In modern society, there is no way for our dogs to keep themselves safe, and thus we are unable to afford them the freedom to meet their own needs. Instead, they must rely on our benevolence for survival.

And our benevolence comes at a price. In exchange for care, we ask our dogs to fill certain roles in our lives. We always have. In the past those roles were ones for which dogs were well equipped. They helped guard and protect us. They helped us tend our farms and hunt for our food. By their very nature, dogs come well prepared for these kinds of physical tasks.

In modern times, however, the work of dogs has become significantly more emotional than physical. We need them to be our comforters, our confidants, our children who never grow up. Meeting the emotional needs of others isn't an easy job. Our dogs are trying, and in large part they are succeeding. The cost, however, appears to be high, as is evidenced by the more than 2.8 million dogs estimated by the American Pet Products Association to be on Prozac or similar psychotropic drugs.

This situation, though far from optimal for our dogs, is unlikely to change any time soon. We must limit some of the freedoms that our dogs might otherwise enjoy—such as running loose at will—in order to keep them safe. In addition, the roles they play in our lives are well established and to a great extent beyond our ability to alter. But there is one thing we can and should control: how we teach our dogs to live alongside us.

When I was growing up in the 1960s and '70s, training your dog meant helping him learn not to go potty in the house. Back then, obedience training for pet dogs was just barely beginning to make its way into the public mindset, and it hadn't yet reached my little corner of Atlanta. But times have changed. Now the outliers are those who do not formally train their dogs. So powerful and pervasive is the idea that one's dog must be obedience-trained that a simple Google search of the phrase *dog training* brings up some 85 million hits.

The idea that as responsible pet parents we must instill obedience in our dogs has become more than just a way to teach them to sit when asked; it has become the very framework for our relationship with them. We treat our dogs largely as we train them. If you believe that dogs must be dominated into submission in order to learn to sit, you will probably be dominating in all that you do with your dog. If you believe that you must continually avoid reinforcing behaviors that you don't want from your dog, then your relationship will be based on the dialectic of reward and punishment. Training ideologies have a pervasive impact on our relationships with our dogs, so it makes sense to examine them carefully.

While there are a myriad of different training techniques out there, the vast majority fall within one of two major camps:

1. Dogs should obey *because I said so*.
2. Dogs' behavior should be controlled through conditioning.

Let's take a closer look at each approach.

Because I Said So (BISS)

Believing that someone must do as you say merely *because you say so* stems largely from the belief that you have a clear right to impose your will on another without taking their thoughts and feelings into consideration. Not only do some dog trainers believe this is acceptable, they argue that demanding blind obedience from a dog is actually in his best interest. While complying with your directives may keep your dog out of trouble at times, it is no way to form a fair and mutually beneficial relationship.

One of the most significant problems with BISS methods is the potential abuse of power. BISS methods convey the idea that it is okay to demand compliance by any means necessary. But methods used to force dogs to obey, such as yelling, leash corrections, and physical punishment, often have serious unintended consequences.

Dr. Meghan Herron and her colleagues at the University of Pennsylvania School of Veterinary Medicine published a groundbreaking study in the journal *Applied Animal Behavior Science* in 2009. The results indicated that using punishment, such as hitting, kicking, yelling, or leash corrections, resulted in a significant increase in aggression by the punished dog.

In parallel, studies have shown that human children who are spanked are significantly more likely to be aggressive toward others than their unspanked peers. And in addition to potentially increasing aggression, using physical punishment on animals who are not able to understand why you are doing so is supremely unfair.

Psychologist Kathy Seifert wrote a column[1] about the trouble with inflicting physical punishment on children in which she relates a story told by Astrid Lindgren, the author of *Pippi Longstocking*. Ms. Lindgren described meeting a pastor's wife, some twenty years earlier, who'd had an illuminating experience with her young son.

Lindgren said that the wife didn't believe in spanking children even though, in those days, spanking kids with a switch — a branch pulled from a tree — was standard punishment. One day, her son of four or five acted out in a way that made her finally believe that she needed to spank him. The mother told her son to go out and find a branch that she could use to hit him. The boy was gone a long time, and when he came back in, he was crying. He said to her, "Mama, I couldn't find a switch, but here's a rock that you can throw at me."

This poor child simply knew his mother needed an instrument with which to cause him pain. If a four- or five-year-old child cannot make the distinction between discipline, designed to encourage him to behave or not behave in certain ways, and retribution, how can we expect a dog to comprehend the difference? The simple answer is that we can't, and therefore, using such methods isn't an acceptable form of training or handling.

BISS methods are inherently damaging to the connection between dog and pet parent. Some methodologies are designed to make us believe that bullying a dog is acceptable, and that fail-

---

[1] Kathy Seifert, PhD, "Spanked! Rethinking Child Discipline," *Stop the Cycle* (blog), *Psychology Today*, July 19, 2012, https://www.psychologytoday.com/blog/stop-the-cycle.

ing to do so actually makes one a bad pet parent. This particular belief system is based on the idea that dogs are so closely related to wolves that we as their guardians should model our methods based on "alpha" wolves.

There are several flaws inherent in this theory. First, there is significant evidence that dogs aren't actually the descendants of wolves but rather that dogs and wolves merely came from a common ancestor. If we assume for the sake of argument that dogs were domesticated from an early model of the gray wolf as some contend, domestication by definition means that significant changes in physiology and behavior have occurred. Additionally, the only wolves easily studied are those living in captivity. Wolves in captivity are most often unrelated, and therefore can be very aggressive in their efforts to achieve status within the group. In the wild, wolves live in family groups where the parents, as leaders, are generally well respected and have little need for overt aggression. Indeed, most researchers agree that the breeding male and female, who used to be called the alphas (researchers no longer commonly use the term since it has been so badly misused in popular culture), are the least likely family members to be aggressive. Interestingly, the actual definition of alpha is "any wolf who lives to be of reproductive age." No mental or physical dominance or bullying required.

Fortunately the alpha model is losing favor and appears to be on its way out as a standard training methodology. Let's hope the other models based on fear and force will quickly follow suit.

Conditioning

The vast majority of animal-training methods in use today, including the popular positive reinforcement movement, are based on the tenets of the behaviorist school of psychology.

The term *behaviorism* was coined by American psychologist John Watson in a 1913 speech at Columbia University that later formed the basis for what was known as the Behaviorist Manifesto. According to Watson, psychologists, as true scientists, should focus exclusively on the study of overt behavior that can be observed and measured. Watson lobbied for psychology to be known as the study of behavior rather than the study of the mind, since he believed the inner workings of the mind, such as thought, feeling, and emotion, to be both unknowable and irrelevant in changing behavior. In the behaviorist model, behaviors are conditioned exclusively through the formation of association between actions and events in the environment.

Russian scientist Ivan Pavlov was a major contributor to the school of behaviorism, though his work actually preceded Watson's manifesto. In the late 1890s, while researching the role of saliva in dogs' digestion, Pavlov made what many referred to as an accidental discovery. First, he noticed that salivation was an unconditioned reflex in the dogs. No prior exposure was required; the salivation just reflexively occurred in the presence of a stimulus that, in the beginning, was the smell or sight of food.

Over the course of several trials, Pavlov noticed that the dogs began to salivate *before* they could actually smell or see food. Upon investigation, he realized that the dogs had become conditioned to the presence of assistants in white lab coats that meant food was on its way, causing them to salivate, a response Pavlov labeled a conditioned reflex. The development of a reflexive response not under voluntary control, such as salivating, based on an environmental stimulus, such as the presence of a white lab coat, is known as respondent or classical conditioning.

Behaviorism Meets Learning

As Pavlov was working on his theory of classical conditioning in the late 1890s, another researcher, this one a psychologist and educator at Columbia University named Edward Thorndike, was studying learning in animals. Thorndike's studies led him to develop what he called the Law of Effect, which states that behavior that is followed by a pleasant consequence is likely to be repeated, while behaviors followed by unpleasant consequences are likely to be stopped.

In the 1930s, the psychologist B. F. Skinner made the next major contribution to the behaviorist movement when he described a form of conditioning that was voluntary rather than reflexive, called operant or instrumental conditioning. Skinner's ideas about operant conditioning led to the development of a behaviorist theory of learning.

According to Skinner's learning theory, we can increase the likelihood of certain behaviors by adding something desirable (positive reinforcement) and by taking something undesirable away (negative reinforcement). We can also decrease the likelihood that a behavior will be repeated through the application of an undesirable stimulus (positive punishment) or through the removal of a desirable stimulus (negative punishment). In dog training, here is what this might look like:

POSITIVE REINFORCEMENT = A reward, such as a treat, is given after the dog obeys a command.

NEGATIVE REINFORCEMENT = The pressure of a pinch collar lessens when the dog stops pulling on the leash.

POSITIVE PUNISHMENT = The dog receives a sharp squeeze from a choke collar for pulling on the leash.

NEGATIVE PUNISHMENT = You stop petting the dog when he jumps on you.

While there is ample evidence of the validity of the behaviorist learning theory, it has led to some rather grim ideas about how best to control the behavior of animals. For example, I receive a weekly email newsletter that recommends various pet products. Often, they're the latest gadgets touted to eliminate problem behaviors, such as excessive barking, through means that include the use of high-pitched sounds that are noxious or even painful to dogs—an example of positive punishment, according to the behaviorist model. Even if these products work to eliminate barking, the cost to your dog, and to your relationship with him, is far too high to make any efficacy relevant. But under the doctrine of strict behaviorism, all that matters is whether or not the response to the dog's behavior works to change that behavior.

I disagree completely with the use of positive punishment as a method of dog training. And I am similarly opposed to the use of *negative reinforcement* techniques, such as hanging a dog by the collar until he is quiet or pinching a dog's ear to encourage him to open his mouth as a method for teaching retrieving, and many people share my view. However, not as many share my opposition to *negative punishments*, such as giving a dog a time-out for rowdy behavior; the *negative punishment* part being removing your attention from him. Still fewer agree when I share my concern about *positive reinforcement*. After all, it's positive, so how can it be bad?

The Negatives of Positive Reinforcement

Nearly twenty years ago, my husband, Kent, a veterinarian, and I sat in a conference room full of service-dog educators gathered to discuss training methods. Best known among the attendees was a woman named Bonnie Bergin, the woman featured in the article my father had read about service dogs and the originator of the concept of using dogs to help people with mobility difficulties. As the discussion turned to operant conditioning, then considered cutting edge in dog training, Bonnie listened with great angst in her expression. "Dogs are capable of so much more than operant conditioning," she insisted. Bonnie's statement, as well as the look on her face, made a vivid impression on me. At the time, we were still using punishment-based training at Canine Assistants, so the idea of using positive reinforcement alone, the trend for those advocating operant conditioning, was novel and appealing, and I embraced it wholeheartedly. It would be years before what Bonnie said actually caused me to reexamine operant conditioning in our own program.

When we let go of force-based techniques at Canine Assistants, we turned to positive reinforcement as our educational methodology. These methods were a vast improvement in numerous ways. Obviously, the approach is kinder and friendlier, allowing both people and dogs to enjoy the process more. The dogs developed strong bonds with their human partners under this methodology. But they also developed extreme anxiety. Why? Positive reinforcement training produced the same consequences as punitive methods. Yes, the process was better, but in the end, we still had dogs who'd been trained to respond to commands— though now we called them cues. The dogs still had no idea how to think or function on their own. Plus, they now had the added pressure of actually liking their human partners and wanting to please them. Worrying about doing the right thing because of the effect that it will have on you is tough enough. Worrying about doing the right thing because you fear disappointing someone you love is pressure on a whole different level.

In retrospect, it seems obvious that this treatment would have made our dogs insecure. Using rewards as the basis for a relationship—offering rewards in exchange for behaviors pleasing to us—is in direct opposition to the concept of unconditional love. The idea that I love you enough to feed you goodies or speak *kindly or scratch your itchy ears but only if you do what I want* did not work well with our dogs. Taking what dogs need or want and using it as a means of manipulating their behavior isn't *positive* for dogs. And it isn't positive for us either. It can be stressful, since in order to avoid marking or rewarding the wrong thing, one must be vigilant and capable of precise timing.

In his bestselling book *Punished by Rewards*, educator and author Alfie Kohn said, "There is a time to admire the grace and persuasive power of an influential idea, and there is a time to fear its hold over us." I'm beginning to be fearful of the hold behaviorism has over the world of dog training. Our dogs, I believe, have concerns of their own.

Worrying About Reinforcement

I was recently in the parking lot outside of PetSmart, about to start my car, when I saw a woman exit with a lovely Doberman at her side. The Dobie's eyes sought her attention with frantic intensity, and the dog seemed desperate for reassurance or, at the very least, some kind of acknowledgment. But the woman didn't seem to notice, and finally, after walking in a perfect heel position for fifty yards, the dog suddenly jumped up on her.

I could tell from watching them that this dog was used to being praised for performing certain behaviors on cue, and that when she wasn't acknowledged, she became worried and sought other ways to gain her mother's attention. At the same time, the dog's training gave the woman tacit approval to ignore her dog, assuming that she would simply *do right* until something called for reprimand. Watching the Dobie leap up on her owner, I had a moment of insight about the problems inherent in current training methods.

But before I could reflect on my epiphany, I saw that the Doberman was about to get in trouble for her behavior, so I popped out of my car, exclaiming, "What a gorgeous Dobie you have!" The woman smiled at me as she commanded the dog, "Off!" I introduced myself and learned that the woman's name was Stephanie and the dog was Annabelle. Annabelle had just returned from two weeks of "boarding school," as Stephanie described it, where she had been trained to behave. Hmm. The result of this schooling seemed to be that Annabelle felt an increased need for attention, while Stephanie felt she no longer had to pay so much attention to her dog now that she had been "properly trained."

Annabelle and Stephanie presented a troubling example of what can happen when we train our dogs to respond only to directives; they require commands in order to function. They can lose the ability to think for themselves, and begin to worry when we don't give them enough feedback.

Similarly, the pressure inherent in positive reinforcement isn't limited to the dogs. It can also increase the pressure on us, as I realized several years ago when I agreed to deliver a service dog trained by another organization to the child with whom he'd been matched in Seattle. I had to make the trip for business anyway, and, since service dogs are allowed to fly in the cabin with their trainers or partners, I looked forward to having the company of a nice dog on the five-hour flight from Atlanta to Seattle.

Redman was a gorgeous male golden, around two years old. I knew he had been trained using only positive reinforcement, so I felt confident that he and I would get along well, and indeed we did—as long as I was directing him. Having moved into Bond-Based Choice Teaching with the Canine Assistants dogs, I was accustomed to partnering with dogs who did not require much direction from me. The typical airplane trip with a Canine Assistants dog usually involved being seated and explaining to the dog that he could relax since the trip would take a while. That was the extent of the guidance I was accustomed to giving. When

I suggested to Redman that he relax, he looked up at me with a panicked expression. That wasn't a cue he understood. So I asked him to sit. He immediately complied but jumped right back up again. For the entire five-hour flight, I had to signal Redman to sit or lie down and stay. When I went more than a minute or two without giving him directions, he panicked. He'd been beautifully trained but he hadn't been taught to function independent of direction. It was a long five hours, but the experience also served as an important reminder of the direct pressure on the person when using positive reinforcement. It is simply far easier to live and work with dogs who have been taught to make good decisions independently rather than those who are trained to comply when cued.

Many modern dog trainers view the tenets of behaviorism as the only science-based methods available. Obviously, utilizing *science-based* methods makes more sense than simply demanding obedience . . . *or else*. But behaviorism is not the only way to educate. Since the late 1950s, other methodologies have largely surpassed behaviorism in the world of early-childhood education, spurred in part by an experiment conducted by American psychologist Harry Harlow, PhD, in 1958.

Behaviorists once believed that infants attached to their mothers simply because the mothers provided them with food. In an effort to test this theory, Dr. Harlow took eight infant rhesus monkeys away from their mothers shortly after birth. He placed each baby in an enclosure with two mother surrogates, one made of wire and the other made of wire covered with cloth. For four of the babies, milk came from the *wire mother,* while the other four got milk from the *cloth mother*. In line with the behaviorist movement, Harlow theorized that the baby monkeys would be most attached to whichever mother surrogate provided the milk.

That didn't happen. All eight of the babies preferred the cloth mothers, for their sense of warmth and security. This indicated that thoughts and feelings, those functions that occur inside the mind, could have an enormous impact on what an animal chooses to do.

Despite Harlow's work and that of others who place importance on the cognitive and emotional processes involved in behavior rather than merely the behavior alone, the works of Watson, Pavlov, and Skinner continue to dominate animal-training methods. Since alternative methods are available but not used, one might conclude that behaviorism remains the best way to work with dogs. But it is not. It's certainly preferable to the BISS approaches, as well as to the so-called Balanced Method, which endeavors to utilize both the BISS approach and conditioning.

While it helps to understand the doctrines of behaviorism, we must look beyond the directly observable when working with dogs. Dogs think and feel. Their internal processes are at least as influential in their decision-making as external stimuli, if not more so. Since dogs are thinking, feeling, social creatures, they need and deserve more than our constant manipulation, whether by threat or reward. The fact that there are millions of dogs out there who have serious stress-related disorders or who are living on psychotropic drugs, including many dogs with whom I've worked in the past at Canine Assistants, compelled me to find a better way.

Two

A Miraculous Shift in Perception

The more I thought about our relationship with dogs, the more determined I became with trying to better it. I knew that changing what we do with our dogs at Canine Assistants simply wasn't enough. It had to go deeper than that. The answer came to me unexpectedly as I recalled a quote from Marianne Williamson's book *A Return to Love: Reflections on the Principles of "A Course in Miracles"*: "A miracle is a shift in perception." In order to relate to our dogs differently, we need to first shift our perception and understand them differently. Once our perception shifts, our actions will logically follow. I began laying the foundation for this new way of understanding our dogs by looking back at how and why we fell in love with dogs in the first place.

Dogs have been domesticated longer than any other species, yet in evolutionary terms, they have existed only for the blink of an eye (there is some debate as to the exact timeframe, but domestic dogs are thought to have evolved from their wolflike ancestor between 18,800 and 32,100 years ago). Nevertheless, there are already estimated to be more than three hundred different breeds and 400 million dogs in the world. How did this happen? Experts have many theories, but I believe the answer is simple. Dogs had us on sight. Man saw dog, man watched dog, man looked dog in the eye . . . and man fell in love with dog.

Animals have always been critical to our survival. They have fed, warmed, frightened, and fascinated us since time began. And in turn, we have honored our sacred connection. In prehistoric times, animals were the focus of cave drawings. Today, they are the focus of books, movies, plays, and songs. Even our language is rich with expressions comparing us to, and even conflating us with, animals. We speak of people as being old goats, blind as bats, young bucks, or strong as an ox. *Biophilia* is the scientific terminology given to our fixation. Harvard biologist Edward O. Wilson defined biophilia as the innately emotional affiliation of human beings to other living organisms. Humans are born biophiliacs.

Imagine what it must have been like for early man. He had to be constantly and acutely aware of the animals in his proximity. They were a powerful force in his life, representing both the opportunity for survival and the very real threat of annihilation. And as man watched these prototype dogs, something began that quite literally changed the course of human existence.

The *mere exposure effect* is a psychological concept suggesting that a person can develop positive feelings toward something just by observing it. Thus, the more often a person sees an animal, such as a dog, the more appealing and likable this animal becomes. Psychologist Robert Zajonc first described this phenomenon in the late 1960s, and it almost certainly accounts for the first critical step in early man's relationship with early dog. We watched dogs, and we started to like what we saw.

Watching dogs also did something more: It allowed us to begin to understand their intentions. Our brain's ability to grasp intentions was first identified by Italian neurophysiologist Giacomo Rizzolatti, PhD, and his team at the University of Parma in the late 1980s, when they implanted electrical sensors into a monkey's motor cortex and discovered that the same neurons fired when the monkey watched someone else carry out a task as fired when the monkey performed the task himself. Dr. Rizzolatti identified this as the function of what he termed *mirror neurons*, which allow us to grasp what is in the minds of others by feeling, rather than thinking. Further studies have determined that humans—and dogs—also have mirror neurons. So as we watched dogs and they watched us, we began to understand one another's intentions, and to read each other emotionally.

We Have Great Chemistry

We share something else with dogs: a chemical known as oxytocin, which is a hormone secreted by the pituitary gland. It is sometimes called the love or cuddle hormone because it's released, among other times, during affectionate physical contact. Oxytocin is also produced when mothers nurse their young, facilitating the bond between mother and child. Oxytocin and related hormones do considerably more for us, as well. They facilitate the building of trust, help reduce pain, and assist in lowering blood pressure. On the flip side, oxytocin is thought to increase our memory of times when trust was broken, which some scientists view as a negative. While this may be reasonable, I contend that since trust makes you vulnerable, a heightened awareness of past betrayals could also be perceived as a positive, protective effect.

The significance of both humans and dogs producing the hormone is that we can increase oxytocin in one another. Many researchers believe that this is the very reason our connection with dogs is so powerful. We are biologically primed to connect.

A study completed at the University of Skövde in Sweden, led by researcher Linda Handlin, determined that pet parents who kiss their dogs frequently have higher levels of oxytocin than those who do not. In addition, they discovered that those who perceived their relationship with their dogs as pleasurable also had higher oxytocin levels. Other studies have indicated that oxytocin increases when people merely look at their dogs for an extended period of time. Perception is, in effect, the key to happiness.

In 2003, South African researchers Johannes Odendaal and Roy Alex Meintjes amazed the scientific community with their findings on the hormones associated with happiness and feelings of well-being, such as phenethylamine, endorphin, dopamine, and oxytocin. These hormones increased and the presence of stress-related hormones, such as cortisol, decreased when people spent just twenty minutes with their dogs. While that wasn't altogether unexpected, the surprise was that the response was virtually identical in the dogs. The feelings and neurochemical effects are mutual, and therein lies the basis for our miraculous shift in perception. We've been treating our dogs as if they are somehow opponents in need of suppressive management. They aren't. They are our allies, whose well-being is intertwined with our own.

Dogs, Like People, Are Highly Social

Dogs and people are highly social creatures. Much of what both species do is dictated by the norms and beliefs of their social group. There is an evolutionary advantage to this kind of socially cooperative behavior: It solidifies the relationships within the pod, thereby making the group stronger. We form social groups, species-blended families, with our dogs. The cluster may consist of a single dog and a single person, or it may include multiple people or animals. Regardless of size, this social grouping gives us the opportunity to use the bonds between members to help dogs learn what constitutes acceptable behavior.

Again from an evolutionary perspective, good leadership

has always been critical for any species to live successfully in social groups. Dogs require our leadership to successfully live in a human-centric world. However, a misunderstanding of what constitutes true leadership has led to abusive forms of dog training, which in turn have gained traction through the popular media. Leadership isn't about coercion; it's about facilitating collaboration. Many scientists who formerly subscribed to the old "survival of the fittest" adage have come to realize that the truth is more likely "survival of the most cooperative." People and dogs, two of the most social, collaborative species on the planet, inhabit virtually every corner of the earth. Our success is not the result of knowing how to fight one another, but rather of knowing how to cooperate with one another.

The studies coming out of canine cognition laboratories in the past twenty years indicate that dogs are capable of much more sophisticated mental processes than we originally believed. Among other things, dogs appear to be able to make inferences, understand labels, categorize certain objects, perform certain quantitative assessments, and understand the concept of a means to an end. Studies also indicate that dogs are capable of empathizing with the situation of another, and they experience a full range of emotions, barring those that require highly sophisticated cognition, such as guilt.

My shift in perception and the new information provided by science gave me the theoretical tenets for my new philosophy. The next step was testing whether the actions dictated by my beliefs would work when applied with our dogs.

Introducing the Bond-Based Approach

The trainer from France who was visiting Canine Assistants began to smile and nod as if she'd just put all the pieces together.

When I asked what she was thinking, she replied haltingly, "This place is a bit of a Crock-Pot for the dogs." Hmm. That was unexpected. It took me a moment to realize that what she'd intended to say was that Canine Assistants was a bit of a pressure cooker, since our dogs have a great deal to learn in a short period of time. She was absolutely right about that. That's what allows us to see the effects of everything we do quickly and clearly. I had the perfect testing grounds at Canine Assistants, and shortly after we began using a Bond-Based approach with our service-dogs-in-training, I knew I was onto something.

But watching the Bond-Based philosophy succeed at Canine Assistants and being brave enough to share it with the rest of the world were two entirely different things. Sometimes new concepts — and this approach is very much a new concept — are met with defensiveness and even derision. So I decided to first present my findings to trainers dedicated to using only force-free methods, as I knew they would be an open-minded audience. A small group of these positive trainers attended a special Teach the Teacher conference I held in the spring of 2014. During the sessions, I explained my new methodology and how we were using it at Canine Assistants.

The trainers were gracious listeners and contributed valuable insights. I was emboldened by their reception, but not yet ready to shout it from the rooftops. After all, this method had been tested only on our very willing service dogs, and though I believed it would work equally well for all dogs, I didn't yet have the research to prove it. Unbeknownst to me, two of the trainers, Judy Luther from St. Louis and Allison Woosley from Louisville, had taken everything discussed at Teach the Teacher and tried it with their pet dog clients. Three months after leaving the conference, Judy called to say that she and Allison were headed back to Atlanta to see me.

When the two women walked into the Canine Assistants

classroom, they appeared elated, and also slightly anxious. The first thing Judy said was, "This is it. This is what we've been missing in the dog world." After a momentary pause, she continued, "Do you know how crazy people are going to think we are? This is very different from everything we've all been taught as dog trainers. . . . But it's like magic. It opens up a whole new world for people and their dogs."

I knew it would take time for people to see the magic in the method, but suddenly I no longer cared what criticism might come. Judy and Allison's excitement and support gave me the confidence I needed to press ahead. It was time to explain to the world that the harmonious, joyful relationships I was seeing at Canine Assistants weren't possible only between working dogs and their handlers. This kind of bond was possible for all dogs and their people. Now I could shout it from the rooftops—or, better yet, write about it in a book!

THE BOND IS THE THING

As I've mentioned, our final examination at Canine Assistants used to involve having service-dog teams perform tasks on command, but we realized that responsiveness to commands did not predict long-term success for our teams. When obedience was emphasized above all else, the bond was sacrificed and the partnership inevitably suffered.

Instead, we found that there is a single predictor of success for our teams at Canine Assistants: the bond between the dog and their person. This is why we call our philosophy Bond-Based. The same will be true for you and your dog. The foundation to a happy life with a well-mannered dog is a strong connection between the two of you. Therefore, your relationship, your social connection to your dog, needs to be at the forefront of your every interaction.

So how do you form a deep and lasting bond with your dog?

Let's begin by defining just what is meant by *bond*. The American Veterinary Medical Association (AVMA) defines the human-animal bond as "a mutually beneficial and dynamic relationship between people and animals that is influenced by behaviors that are essential to the health and well-being of both." From this definition, we can discern three key components:

1. The bond should be mutually beneficial.
2. The bond should always remain a *work in progress*.
3. The health and well-being of both species impacts the bond between the two.

YOU + ME = WE

When I was pregnant with my son, Chase, several people warned me that once he arrived, I would no longer love my animals with the same level of intensity I felt for them in my pre-child years. Chase is now twelve and I'm still waiting for that to happen. I'm sure that it never will. But it troubles me to consider: Do people really think of dogs as placeholders for something missing in their lives, whether a child or a spouse or even a job? As I considered the possibilities, I realized that most human-dog relationships fall into one of three categories:

1. **The MEs:** Those people who do use dogs to fill a void in their life, often until something perceived as better comes along. Sometimes, these people also attribute adult human characteristics, along with very high expectations, to their dogs.
2. **The THEEs:** Those who use dogs for the things they can do, such as personal protection, livestock guarding, hunting, etc.
3. **The WEs:** Those who have a relationship with their dogs based on respect, understanding, and admiration,

the result of which is mutually beneficial. Luckily,
some MEs and THEEs can also be (or become) WEs.

We should not use our dogs as practice children, or as place-holders of any kind. It isn't fair to them. It puts them at risk for being shunted aside when the real deal comes along and we don't need them anymore. In addition, people who view their dogs with unrealistic expectations can often react badly when a dog acts like a dog. This does not mean that it is wrong to use the child-parent model in caring for our dogs. Dogs can be, and are, our children who never leave home. But they cannot be our children of *convenience*. Likewise, we should not use dogs solely for what they can do for us. What happens when they get too old to do for us anymore? All dogs are WEs. Once dogs fall in love with people, their bond is unwavering, resolute, and eternal. It's a life lesson from our dogs that we would do well to emulate.

Why Is Choice Important for Our Dogs?

Dogs don't get to make a lot of choices. They can't feed themselves, and we get upset when they try. We choose their toys and their playmates. We determine when and how much they are allowed to vocalize. On walks, we try to control how fast they go, where they go, and even what they sniff. In some ways, taking more control over the lives of dogs is a good thing. Since they must live in a human-dominated world, it's safer for them to be treated like toddlers. Their environment makes it virtually impossible for them to fend for themselves. But at the same time, we have made them toddler-like without also giving them the consideration we provide young children. We expect dogs to be totally dependent and obedient, while also expecting them to be responsible for their own actions. We insist that they know it's never okay to eat food off the kitchen counter or chew on shoes. We think they should be capable of staying alone for extended periods of time without toileting or displaying any self-soothing displacement behaviors, such as table leg chewing, door panel scratching, or toilet paper shredding. It's illogical to try to control everything our dogs do and then expect them to be responsible for their own behavior. Dogs must live in our world without opposable thumbs or the ability to read street signs, but we should allow them as much choice and independence as we possibly can.

There are two primary reasons why choice is such an important part of how we interact with our dogs. First, giving your dog a sense of control, the ability to make his own choices, is critical for his well-being. There is nothing more terrifying, for dogs or humans, than believing that you cannot affect your circumstances. Second, there are times when our dogs have to be responsible for their own actions and must be able to make their own choices, such as when left home alone.

Training can be defined in many different ways. But it's important to note that *training* your dog is the opposite of giving him the ability to *choose*. For the purposes of this book, I am defining training as the process of eliciting a particular behavioral response, absent the need of independent thought, to an environmental cue usually provided by a person. Since it's obvious that you cannot be with your dog all the time to provide cues and control his behavior, it's necessary to stop training and begin actually teaching our dogs to think and make good choices on their own.

TRADING REWARD AND PUNISHMENT FOR SOCIAL LEARNING

While conditioning via reinforcement and punishment can be effective, in the sense that this approach can get a dog to do what we want him to do, it is an approach that can cause immense stress for a dog. While it is entirely possible to contort all behaviors to make them fit the model of reward and punishment, it behooves us to stop manipulating our dogs' behavior through training and instead begin focusing on helping them learn how to behave appropriately.

Are there times when we have to tell our dogs what to do? Absolutely. I'm in no way saying that we should let our dogs do whatever they want, whenever they want. None of us can operate that way and survive. But since we know that dogs are highly social and that they consider us part of their social group, it makes sense to use a social, relationship-based approach to help them understand what to do in a given situation.

Imagine you are speeding down the road and the driver of an oncoming car leans out the window and screams, "Slow down!" You would likely be irritated by the directive and perhaps even speed up a bit. But if that same driver flashed his headlights as he passed, you'd slow down willingly, recognizing the social signal that a police car was nearby. If that same light-flashing scenario was repeated week after week until one day the other driver didn't flash his lights but rather yelled "Slow down," you'd instantly reduce your speed, now trusting the other driver as having your best interests at heart. That trust would also make you willing to do almost anything else this driver might ask of you.

When working with dogs, commands are the equivalent of yelling "Slow down," while providing information in a social format such as demonstration (described in more detail in Chapter Seven) is the equivalent of flashing our headlights. The more we can flash our proverbial lights, the more likely our dogs are to listen if we ever need to yell "Slow down!"

Love Is All You Need

There is really just one thing that's necessary to successfully apply the knowledge I'll give you in the following chapters: love. It's something our dogs already give us. There is a Dave Barry quote that says, "You can say any fool thing to a dog and the dog will give you this look that says, 'My GOSH, you're RIGHT! I NEVER would've thought of that!'" It's true. If a dog loves you, he will look at you as if anything that comes out of your mouth is brilliant. While some may consider this a demonstration of the dog's lack of intellectual discernment, I see it as proof of the unconditional nature of a dog's love. Your dog doesn't think, *I will love you if you are brilliant*; he just loves you. Because he loves you, your brilliance, in his eyes, is a given. Our dogs have learned the secret power of loving unconditionally. Now it's our opportunity to return that love.

We've been complicating things unnecessarily, training our dogs in an effort to make them lovable to us. But it's really much simpler than that. The love needs to come first. Dogs who are loved love in return, allowing a strong bond to develop. Within that bond lies the desire to see the person they love happy. Dogs who know they are loved feel safe enough to learn to make good choices. And while the payoff for loving our dogs is enormous, that must never be our focus. Dogs don't make us earn their love and we shouldn't make them earn ours. Love, freely given, is what makes Bond-Based Choice Teaching possible.

So, you bring the love and I'll supply the knowledge. We can trust your dog to do the rest.

Three

Pet Parenting

My friend Judy says the dogs at Canine Assistants are "fertile ground for learning." I like to believe that's true. We work hard to prepare our dogs for the many challenges that they might experience as service dogs throughout their lives, such as the need to find help in an emergency, with confidence. While, of course, part of our job involves educating our dogs, it's necessary to first make certain they are completely confident that their own needs will be met. We must parent them.

Actually, in some cases, we begin by *parenting* their parents.

Sweet Louise

I've loved Louise and her sister, Thelma, since I first held them in my arms just moments after they were born. What a pair. They were a litter of just two golden retriever puppies, but Thelma and Louise had personalities that could fill a room, and the rowdy little girls quickly grew into stunning adults. Thelma graduated as a service dog, finding her one true love in an amazing young woman from Kentucky. Louise was placed with a volunteer family as a breeder, charged with the responsibility of providing us with our next generation of wonder dogs. (For more information on why we have a breeding program, please see Appendix A.)

I remember so clearly the day that Louise arrived at Canine Assistants, ready to give birth to her fourth and final litter for us, after which she would be spayed and placed permanently in the care of her volunteer family. She was the only female to be bred all four times to the same male, Butch, the goldendoodle. Since Butch lived with me, I considered Louise my daughter-in-law. The puppies from their three previous litters were everything I could have hoped for in working dogs—kind and gentle like their mother, and smart, willing, and occasionally laugh-out-loud funny like their father.

An ultrasound done at twenty-eight days had shown that she was indeed pregnant with at least a few puppies. Though she remained with her volunteer family until the end of her pregnancy, I thought about her daily. It was fun explaining to my son where the puppies would be in the developmental process: inch-long embryos at thirty days; fetuses at thirty-nine, about the same time their ears become visible and eyelids have formed; and finally, over the last three weeks, recognizably puppy-like creatures, with claws and fur.

As Louise neared her due date, sixty-three days after breeding, she came to Canine Assistants to settle into her delivery room. The delivery room at Canine Assistants is actually a round, custom-made tub under the glass top of a desk in the veterinary clinic. A radiograph confirmed that Louise was carrying four puppies, a small litter for a golden, but I was excited nonetheless.

We carefully observe our moms-to-be prior to whelping, checking their temperatures multiple times in an effort to catch the drop that signals decreasing progesterone, a sign that delivery is imminent. My husband, ever the veterinarian, continually monitored her progress. With this litter, we were all particularly eager and a little more anxious than usual. This was an important batch of puppies for us, the last of a very successful breeding combination. We certainly didn't want anything to go wrong. Those four babies were priceless.

On the day Louise arrived at Canine Assistants, she appeared to be several days from delivery, according to both her breeding record and her temperature chart. So we were shocked when our farm manager called the very next morning to tell us that he'd found four healthy babies in Louise's tub when he went to take her out on her first walk of the day. Sweet Louise had delivered alone, and she had done it perfectly. There were three girls and one boy, each adorable.

We named the three girls Mazzie, Moxie, and Mischief, and we named the boy Mojo. They are collectively known as the M&M litter, four furry bundles of heroic possibility. Louise took care of their needs until they began eating kibble at three weeks of age, when we began helping with her parental duties. By the time the puppies were five weeks old, Louise was ready to go home and for us to take over the parenting. It was a role for which we'd been preparing since long before the babies were born.

Epigenetics

In the past twenty years, a new buzzword has emerged in the nature-versus-nurture debate: *epigenetics*. *Epigenetic* literally means "above the gene," and epigenetics is the study of how external experiences affect the expression of genetic traits without actually changing the genetic sequence. An epigenetic change is like a sticky note attached to the outside of a gene, with instructions for cells on exactly how to use that gene. An analogy may make this easier to comprehend. Imagine you rent a pre-furnished home with roommates. Those furnishings are the fixed potential of the house, much like your genetic sequence is the fixed potential of your body. Epigenetics are like a sticky note placed on the thermostat that says, "Heat may be turned on only when the temperature goes below 65°F." The note changes nothing about the equipment itself, it only impacts when and how you use it.

It is likely that an external factor caused you to place this note on the thermostat—perhaps you're between jobs and that's why you want to prevent your roommates from running up the heating bill. The experiences you have, the choices you make, the influence of those around you—those are all factors that go into the creation of these small epigenetic sticky notes. It seems that experiences affect the way our cells interpret our genetic code, meaning that nature and nurture are more closely intertwined than previously thought.

Scientists used to think that epigenetic changes were specific only to an individual and were not passed on to his or her progeny. But geneticists now believe that this isn't precisely true. It seems that some epigenetic changes can be passed from parent to offspring. This is enormous news, because it means that our life experiences and lifestyle choices may well affect our children, grandchildren, and generations to come. For example, if a traumatic experience lowers someone's genetic threshold, or trigger point, for depression, then that lower trigger point may be passed on to future generations. The same holds true for dogs, meaning that the first and most important thing we must do for puppies is make certain that their parents are well socialized and truly loved, in addition to being genetically healthy. Louise fits that description beautifully.

Nursery Pups

Our puppies spend the first few days of life under that glass-topped desk in the veterinary clinic. Once the puppies begin gaining weight, they are moved with their mother to the nursery house, where volunteers, under the guidance of a resident staffer, begin caring for them. Lack of weight gain is often the first sign that a puppy isn't doing well, so each is weighed twice a day until we are confident that normal progress is being made. In addition to weighing them, we monitor the puppies carefully to be certain that they are developing normally, using the following developmental phases as our guideline. (For more information on the Canine Assistants Nursery, please see Appendix B.)

THE NEONATAL PERIOD

For puppies, this phase extends from birth through thirteen days of age. The two important objectives for puppies during this period are to stay warm and to receive nutrition. Neonatal puppies must stay close to their mom and littermates, since that is the only way they can control their body temperature. They cannot see or hear at this point and have a somewhat limited ability to smell, though some experts believe neonatal puppies can recognize the smell of their mothers, toward whom they often crawl in circular patterns. At this age, puppies must rely on stimulation from their mom to urinate and defecate. Though their bodies are growing at a rapid rate during this stage, their brain waves show little difference between when they are awake and when they are asleep.

THE TRANSITION PERIOD

The next phase extends from day fourteen of life through day twenty-eight, during which time puppies go through significant physical changes but remain close to Mom and littermates. They begin opening their eyes around day thirteen, though they cannot see objects or detect motion until their retinas have become more developed, around day twenty-one. Ear canals begin to open, and by day eighteen or so, they react to sounds, though they can't localize the origin of the noises until toward the end of the period.

During the early part of this phase, puppies begin to crawl and take their first wobbly steps. Often, puppies show their first tail wags, although those wags are believed to be merely signs of development rather than deliberate responses to sensory stimulation. By their fourth week of life, the puppies will begin interactive play, which will be a huge part of their lifelong learning and development. They get their first teeth at the beginning of the transitional phase, and by the end, they will be eating solid food and no longer require Mom's help with toileting. These small teeth are razor sharp and will be used for things other than eating, such as biting littermates and Mom. Those actions will result in a puppy's first experience with corrective behaviors from other dogs.

THE SOCIALIZATION PERIOD

By weeks four through twelve, the puppies are starting to look like real dogs. They learn to move with increasing coordination, even attempting clumsy runs and jumps. While they still want to nurse and play with Mom, especially early in this period, much of their focus is on interactions with their littermates and the people in their lives. This period marks the beginning of the time when puppies learn what is normal and acceptable behavior, so positive exposures are essential.

We begin taking our puppies on very short outings with their littermates when they are about five weeks old. Initially, the puppies are carried in slings or strollers, since they have little immunity until after their second set of vaccinations, at around nine weeks old. Home visits with volunteers also start during this time, with the rule being that two puppies must go to a volunteer's home together, or the volunteer must sleep with a single puppy. This is done so that the puppies always have the emotional security of close proximity to either their human or a littermate. Our puppies do seem to dip through a short fearful period beginning at approximately eight weeks, and we try to be mindful of this stage, giving them extra confidence-building experiences such as letting them find pieces of kibble hidden in the grass.

The first several months of life are as formative for puppies as they are for human babies, so our focus must be on providing them with as many enjoyable experiences and exposures as possible. Our goal with these experiences is twofold. We must help the puppies learn to socialize appropriately with the people and animals with whom they might interact in adulthood. And we must help them habituate to those environments in which they will find themselves in the future. (For more information on the Canine Assistants socialization and habituation protocol, please see Appendix C, "Raising Canines.")

With humans, we know that a lack of exposure to stimuli in early childhood impedes normal brain development,[1] and many of the delays caused by sensory deprivation in children appear to be permanent despite the fact that the human brain is not fully developed until approximately twenty-five years of age. In puppies, there is even less time to support positive brain development, since approximately 80 percent of a dog's brain is developed by four months of age, with the remaining 20 percent completed by one year.[2]

It is particularly important for dogs to develop trust in humans and confidence in themselves at an early age, so we begin spending a great deal of time with them when they are four or five weeks old. Though it's easiest to begin the process of social-

[1] Carolyn Y. Johnson, "Scientists Begin to Unravel the Long-Lasting Biological Effects of Early-Life Adversity, Social Isolation," September 21, 2012, Boston.com, http://www.boston.com/news/science/2012/09/21/scientists-begin-unravel-the-long-lasting-biological-effects-early-life-adversity-social-isolation/j28yh2lHWj3P8vYY1CpGPO/story.html.
[2] Ray Coppinger and Lorna Coppinger, *Dogs: A Startling New Understanding of Canine Origin, Behavior, and Evolution* (New York: Scribner, 2001).

ization when puppies are young, dogs of all ages can develop this type of trust and confidence.

Fostering Secure Attachment

In the past fifteen years or so, multiple studies have indicated that dogs form relationships with their primary caregivers that are surprisingly similar to those that human infants form with their primary parent. Therefore, it's important to understand something about human attachments if we are to have the best possible relationships with our dogs.

After World War II, British psychologist John Bowlby developed a psychological model called *attachment theory* that is still used today. Dr. Bowlby believed that a child's need for attachment comes from his need for safety, and that the fundamental nature of the early bond a child forms with his primary caregivers has a lifelong impact on his emotional well-being. Bowlby listed four characteristics of secure attachment:

- *Proximity Maintenance:* The child's desire to stay close to caregiver.
- *Safe Haven:* The child running back to the caregiver when frightened or uncertain.
- *Secure Base:* The caregiver forming a stable base from which the child can explore his environment.
- *Separation Distress:* The child feeling mild anxiety when caregiver is not present.

In the 1970s, developmental psychologist Mary Ainsworth built on Bowlby's original work through her "Strange Situation" study of children twelve to eighteen months of age and their interactions with their parents. Dr. Ainsworth identified three major styles of attachment, based on what she observed:

- *Secure Attachment:* Marked by separation distress when children were away from caregivers and joy when reunited with them. Securely attached children seek comfort from their caregivers in times of need, comfortable in the knowledge that they will promptly provide reassurance.
- *Ambivalent-Insecure Attachment:* Marked by distress when a caregiver leaves and inconsistent reactions, such as anger one time and joy the next, upon being reunited with the caregiver. This attachment style is thought to be the result of the lack of availability on the part of early caregivers.
- *Avoidant-Insecure Attachment:* These children show no preference between caregivers and total strangers and tend to be altogether emotionally withdrawn. This style is thought to be the result of punishment or abuse, and these children have learned not to seek reassurance from caregivers.

In the mid-1980s, researchers Mary Main and Judith Solomon added a fourth style to Ainsworth's original three.

- *Disorganized-Insecure Attachment:* Represents children whose attachment styles change frequently. This attachment pattern is thought to be the result of inconsistent behavior on the part of caregivers, such that they may be the sources of both comfort and fear. It has been repeatedly shown that this type of attachment puts children at risk for high levels of hostility and aggression later in life.

Though Bowlby described attachment as a "lasting psychological connectedness between human beings," studies done with dogs have shown that attachment theory applies to the human-canine bond as well. Researchers have conducted multiple studies based on Ainsworth's Strange Situation test, revealing that dogs play and explore more when their owners are present than when left alone or with a stranger, and they seek more contact with their owners than with strangers when each returns from an absence. Dogs were also found to have lower heart rate spikes when exposed to frightening stimuli while their caregivers where present.

In 2013, the scientific journal *PLOS ONE* published one of the most compelling studies of dogs and Bowlby's secure-base effect, by Lisa Horn and her colleagues at the University of Veterinary Medicine in Vienna. Dr. Horn provided dogs with toys that could be manipulated to produce a food reward, then examined their reactions under three conditions: when their owner was absent, when their owner was present but silent, and when the owner was present and encouraging the dog to interact with the toys. Dogs were found to be much less interested in trying to get the food reward when their owners were absent. No real difference was seen in the dogs' efforts when owners were silent versus encouraging. In a follow-up study, Horn replaced owners with strangers, finding that the dogs had little interaction with the strangers and were not interested in pursuing the food rewards in their presence. The researchers concluded that the presence of the owners was important for the dogs to behave in a confident manner, the defining characteristic of the secure-base component in Bowlby's original attachment theory.

So there are clear parallels between the types of attachment seen in children and those discerned in dogs. Interestingly, while attachment theory holds that children form a level of confidence based on the early behavior of caregivers that remains fairly consistent throughout their lives, dogs remain comparatively childlike throughout their lives, suggesting that even those who don't have secure attachments in puppyhood can still find them later in life.

Here is my version of Bowlby's attachment theory, modified for dogs:

- *Proximity Maintenance:* Securely attached dogs seek to stay close to their people most of the time.
- *Safe Haven:* When alarmed, securely attached dogs will seek the protection of their people.
- *Secure Base:* A secure attachment to their people allows dogs to explore and try new things, knowing their people will always be available to them if needed.
- *Separation Distress and Reunion Joy:* Securely attached dogs do not want their people to leave them, often whining or barking when they go. They will settle down after a relatively short period of time, typically under thirty minutes. This is a significant distinction between appropriate separation distress and true separation anxiety for a dog, a condition that requires professional help.

Stages of Canine Attachment

Now that we know *what* behaviors we should see in dogs, we need to know *when* to expect them. Just as John Bowlby found that there are separate stages of child-parent attachment in humans, we can discern clear stages in attachment for dogs.

Pre-Attachment

IN CHILDREN: Birth through six to twelve weeks. At this young age, infants do not show a marked preference for a particular caregiver.

IN PUPPIES: Birth until approximately four to five weeks of age. During this time, puppies are focused exclusively on biological survival. Adult dogs who haven't had positive experiences with people also seem to experience this same phase. When these adult dogs (which I call *reborns*) enter safe relationships with people for the first time, for several weeks they can focus only on survival, like newborn puppies. Reborns need to be reassured that their biological needs of food, water, and shelter will be met. Otherwise, reborns should be left alone, with the exception of positive interactions with their primary caregiver, during this period and allowed to acclimate to their new environment without external stressors.

Indiscriminate Attachment

IN CHILDREN: The pre-attachment phase ends as children begin to show a desire to connect with others, and thus are considered to have entered the indiscriminate attachment phase. During this time, children get better at distinguishing individuals. While they will normally accept care from others, they prefer to be with their primary and secondary caregivers, some showing an obvious preference exclusively for their primary caregiver in this period. This phase lasts until approximately seven months of age.

IN PUPPIES: After four to five weeks, when they have developed the ability to eat kibble, toilet independently, and move with relative ease, they enter an indiscriminate attachment period of their own. While they may love their primary and secondary caregivers, most puppies seem willing and able to attach to all people until they reach roughly twenty weeks of age. Most reborns do not experience this indiscriminate attachment phase.

Discriminate Attachment

IN CHILDREN: This period lasts from around seven to eleven months of age. During this time, children begin to show a decided preference for one individual and display separation anxiety when taken from this individual, as well as "stranger anxiety."

IN PUPPIES: Beginning at approximately four months of age, puppies also show discriminate attachment to one person (possibly two people). While puppies of this age may be willing to work and play with multiple people, stressful situations are best handled by the primary caregiver(s). Reborns enter this discriminate attachment period as their confidence in the security of their environment increases. The length of time it takes to reach this point varies significantly based on multiple factors, such as a dog's background. Some reborns are ready to bond to multiple people within months, while others need much longer. The best course of action is to make sure all people involved in the dog's life behave as benevolent caregivers, allowing the dog to form bonds as he seeks them.

Multiple Attachment

IN CHILDREN: After nine to twenty months of age, they enter the multiple attachment phase and begin to form bonds with caregivers other than their primary parent. These bonds can include other parents, siblings, grandparents, and babysitters. These relationships appear to be predictive of the relationships they will form as older children and adults.

IN PUPPIES: At around eight to twelve months, they enter the multiple attachment phase and begin to show a willingness to form relationships with more than one or two people. These relationships are not the superficial affinity seen when puppies are young, but rather much deeper bonds that require careful cultivation.

Now that we know what secure attachment looks like and when to expect it, the next logical question to ask is how we can best facilitate it. To answer this, it again helps to look at parenting styles with human children.

Authoritative parenting is based on the idea that parents should establish clear boundaries for behavior and then work with their children to help them make appropriate decisions. Unlike "helicopter parents," who control every moment of their children's lives, authoritative parents act as guides, encouraging children to express opinions and develop an appropriate degree of independence.

Attachment parenting rests on the idea that parents and children must form a strong emotional bond, helping the child to become a more secure, empathic, peaceful human being. Attachment parents believe that friendship is an important part of parenting. They also believe that children have valuable skills and opinions and should at times be allowed to lead rather than follow.

At Canine Assistants, we have combined elements from these two parenting models into what we call Benevolent Pet Parenting. Under this method, a secure attachment bond between human and dog forms the basis for appropriate behavior throughout the dog's life. There is a Maya Angelou quote that I find equally applicable to dogs as it is to people: "I've learned that people will forget what you said, people will forget what you did, but people will never forget how you made them feel." Just like people, our dogs never forget how we make them feel.

One of my all-time favorite dogs is an Australian shepherd named Rusty. Rusty was diagnosed with multiple malignant masses on one of his front legs. The oncologists told Rusty's human mom that he would need extensive radiation treatment in order to survive. Rusty had to be sedated for the treatments, which resulted in burns so extensive it looked as if the skin had been peeled off his leg. The process could not have been fun for

Rusty, yet he was so excited to go to the Cancer Treatment Center for each session that he was difficult to restrain. How could he have such good feelings about such an awful process? Clare, the technician who managed Rusty's care, made Rusty feel safe and loved, and the pleasure of those feelings trumped the pain of the procedure.

It isn't simply when our dogs are experiencing difficult times, like Rusty's radiation treatments, that we need to be focused on making them feel good about themselves. When a dog lives in a state of constant dependency on us for survival, this can easily turn into a near-constant state of fear: Can I please my person? Will they feed me? Are they coming home? Am I capable? We must ensure that the answer to these questions is YES! In order to help a dog be truly exceptional, whether during a brief teaching session or for the whole of his life, you must help him feel secure enough to trust you and confident enough to trust himself.

Ways You Can Help Your Dog Feel Secure and Confident

SHARE YOUR FOOD

Bess was a young golden retriever who could not seem to relax anywhere but her kennel room or a crate. When with people, she would pace and pant and generally seemed miserable. She was extremely kind and attentive, but she wasn't happy. No matter who was nearby, she stayed on red alert. I had no idea how to help her, so my only hope was to bring in my son, Chase, the only person I knew who could possibly connect with Bess. Chase was only twelve years old at the time, but he already "spoke dog," instinctually knowing what dogs want and need better than anyone I've known.

Chase watched Bess for a few minutes and then asked my permission to try something that we don't usually do. I agreed, and Chase briefly left the small office where we'd gathered with Bess, returning with an iCalm (an iPod-like device that plays a music program created to relax dogs, a system we will discuss in more detail in Chapter Four) and a paper plate stacked with various cheeses and meats. Leaving the iCalm playing softly and the plate within reach on a nearby table, Chase sat on the floor and called Bess to him.

After a few minutes of gently massaging her ears, he retrieved the plate of treats and did something that would cause most traditional dog trainers great consternation. He took a bite of the food, then handed a bite to Bess, and continued sharing this way until all the food was gone. Afterward, he went back to massaging in gentle circles while smiling, speaking softly, and making brief but frequent eye contact for about two minutes at a time. He took a deep breath and audibly sighed as he exhaled, relaxing all his muscles. Bess lay down for the first time in the four hours we'd been working with her, and within minutes she was deeply asleep.

I was astounded. Though only twelve, Chase showed remarkable insight into dogs. He was instinctively using food sharing to quickly form a small social group of two, creating a caregiving bond with Bess that would allow him to influence how she was feeling. Once Bess trusted Chase, he could guide her into understanding that it was safe to relax. It was an excellent example of the power of social learning, in the broadest sense of the term—learning what to do from another in your social group. Food sharing, in small amounts with food safe for dogs, is now a technique we use frequently. This practice does not encourage them to beg for food. In fact, numerous reports have indicated that food sharing actually reduces begging and the taking of food without permission. Since we began food sharing, my own dog Jack, once an accomplished thief of any food accidentally left within his reach, now routinely brings me any edibles he finds as if requesting permission to eat. Jack no longer has to steal. He has merely to ask. Perhaps the more open we are with our dogs, the more open they can be with us.

SPEND TIME TOGETHER

While dogs may not be pack animals from a biological perspective, they are highly social, requiring the company of others, at least a good bit of the time, to be happy. The vast majority of dogs prefer the company of their beloved humans to anyone, even to other dogs in the family. Every positive interaction you have with your dog fosters his trust in you. These communal interactions may be subtle, and include sharing eye contact, scratching, massaging, grooming, and snuggling. But they may also be more active and include playing, walking, and any other activity that involves positive physical contact between you and your dog.

While I believe it is vital that dogs be socially comfortable around other dogs, they don't have to spend time with other dogs to be socially fulfilled. If your dog does enjoy canine contact, by all means give him ample opportunity to play with other dogs. Conversely, if he does not seem to truly enjoy interacting with other dogs, then cross the dog park off your list of places to play. Remember, time with you is what your dog craves most.

LET HIM KNOW YOU ARE HAPPY WITH HIM

At Canine Assistants, we raise our dogs to believe that people are worthy of their affection. Such devotion leads them to care deeply about how we feel toward them—a very vulnerable position. Many pet dogs are in the same vulnerable position. Everyday life is filled with affection—until the dog does something that the human deems *inappropriate*, at which time the human responds by withdrawing attention or affection. This must be terrifying for dogs whose very lives depend on our benevolence.

One of the greatest threats to our dogs' peace of mind is the worry that we are somehow not happy with them. Many times the problem behaviors we see in dogs, such as submissive urination, grabbing arms, nipping human skin, and jumping up on people, are actually caused by anxiety and fear that we will not or do not love them enough. It must be difficult to be so totally dependent on the kindness of others for survival. And, as discussed, we've intensified their dependence on us by increasing our level of caregiving toward them. So we must be vigilant not to confuse our dogs with unreasonable expectations or punishments that they simply cannot understand.

Children who have a strong connection to their parents worry about disappointing them. Older children are able to understand that when a parent is upset with them it doesn't mean that they are no longer loved. However, younger children—and dogs—simply can't make this distinction. Social species are designed to worry about the well-being and happiness of those with whom they have bonded.

BE PRESENT

Just being present physically and mentally, as often as possible, goes a long way toward creating a strong relationship. So often, dogs are the losers in our multitasking world. We feed them while we're on the phone. We walk them while listening to our iPods. We brush them while watching television. Sometimes it's important to spend time simply being with your dog.

Touching your dog facilitates bonding by producing oxytocin and other hormones associated with attachment. Allow your dog to show you where and how he likes to be petted. Most dogs love being scratched at the base of the tail or on the chest. Don't restrain your dog while petting him—make him a voluntary participant. Light touches tend to excite the nervous system; conversely, deep pressure relaxes the nervous system.

Making eye contact with your dog can also stimulate the production of hormones associated with bonding. Keep your eyes soft and avoid staring in any way that might seem threatening to your dog. Tilt your head slightly to one side and lower your chin to appear less intimidating. Encourage your dog to make eye contact by saying his name or making a noise that gains his attention. Maintain the contact for three to five seconds if possible while speaking in a soothing tone. If your dog is shy about holding eye contact, begin with quick glances and build duration slowly. Initially, eye contact is about facilitating attachment. As your bond strengthens, you and your dog will be able to use that contact to communicate a myriad of thoughts and feelings.

Softly spoken words of affection go a long way toward establishing a connection between you and your dog. Not only is it important to speak to your dog kindly, it's important that you try to imagine what your dog is thinking and feeling and what he might say to you about it if he could. This exercise, verbalizing our dogs' thoughts, can help us develop patience and empathy toward them. It isn't even important that you accurately translate your dog's mindset, just that you remain aware that your dog has thoughts and feelings. Personally, I hear my dogs in my mind frequently. They say lovely things about me.

As we reach adulthood, it's sometimes difficult to remember to take time to play. Fortunately, we have dogs to help remind us. Playing with your dog is a fun way to create a connection, whether playing fetch, hide-and-seek, or my personal favorite, tug-of-war. In the past, many trainers mandated that people must *win* the tug-of-war game in order to keep their dogs from feeling they achieved an upper hand in the relationship. But recent studies have shown that dogs who play tug-of-war, whether they win or lose, *are more responsive to their handler* than those who do not. My personal tug-of-war record against my goldendoodle, Butch, is 0–1,168. I'm a graceful loser.

FEED YOUR DOG'S NEED FOR AFFECTION

Some years back, there was a four-month-old Canine Assistants puppy named Joy who'd been confined to her crate for several weeks because of an eye injury. There was a note on the top of her crate that read "If Joy jumps on you, please ignore her." Since this was before my enlightenment, this was the response I'd always suggested to my staff, the theory behind which was that you should never *reward* behavior you don't want to see repeated. But as I read the note and looked at the sweet puppy, I realized how wrong I'd been. If a dog jumps up in order to connect with a person, she should not be ignored. Rather, we must *feed the need* of the dog by using both hands to massage her, while giving her complete attention.

We call the act of being supremely attentive to our dogs Two Hands, All In, and it's a method we use whenever our dogs are anxious or needy. It can be applied literally by putting both of your hands on your dog, or figuratively in a situation when you can't make physical contact or it might not be wise to do so—such as with a dog you don't know well or one who doesn't feel comfortable being touched—by blocking out all distractions and focusing solely on the dog.

I'm certain that the idea of feeding the need will sound like blasphemy to many dog trainers. But in every case where a dog's problematic behavior is the result of an emotional need, it's our obligation to fill that need, providing him with the security he's searching for. It simply isn't fair to punish a dog who's asking for our affection by *withholding* affection, just as it wouldn't be reasonable to ignore a toddler who hugs us. The same goes for dogs who grab our arms or jump up on us as a means of establishing contact. If that contact hurts, by all means *yipe* loudly to alert your dog to the hurt, but don't ignore him. And don't withdraw your affection simply because he was a little toothy or overly zealous in his greeting.

Before you can help your dog develop a more acceptable way to establish a connection with you, you must meet his underlying needs. Doing otherwise in the name of not reinforcing bad behavior is not only unfair, it's ineffective in the long run. If your dog's emotional needs are not met, he may begin displaying other problematic behaviors, such as chewing his feet or pulling out clumps of fur.

I'm convinced that it's our withholding of affection that has made attention-seeking behaviors, such as jumping up on people, so prevalent and difficult to extinguish. If you feed your dog's emotional need when he jumps on you until he willingly puts his paws back on the ground, without forcing him down right away or scolding him, he will jump less and less frequently, because he will be increasingly secure in your attachment to him. I have tested this theory with hundreds of dogs now and have yet to see it fail.

If you cannot physically withstand jumpy or mouthy greetings, go Two Hands, All In before he jumps or hold a toy out for him to take one end of while you hold the other end. To keep your dog from jumping or mouthing on guests in greeting, feed his emotional needs by giving him some form of reassuring physical contact, such as stroking his ears or rubbing under his jaw, until you sense that he is at ease. Once he settles, you can try letting your guest take over the patting, but keep in mind that this may hype him up again and that your guest will need to keep the touches going until your dog once again relaxes.

I realize this advice may go against what you've heard before. This is a new approach for dog parents, as it once was for human parents. In the past, the parents of new babies were frequently told not to pick up their children when they cried, since doing so would make the babies more likely to cry in the future in an effort to gain attention. Mercifully, the philosophy fell out of favor when parents and parenting experts realized that comforting crying infants actually makes them less likely to cry in the future.

Babies who have their needs met don't need to cry for attention. Likewise, dogs who have their emotional and social needs met stop jumping, mouthing, and making other such efforts far more quickly than those who are corrected or redirected when they seek attention.

The old adage is, "A tired dog is a good dog." While physical and mental exercise are of vital importance, I believe the saying should be "A *securely attached* dog is a good dog."

Four

Friends Indeed

When our dogs love us, they study us carefully, watching to learn how we see the world, what makes us happy, and what upsets us. They so embody the spirit of friendship that they've earned the label *man's best friend*. It's a moniker that is hard earned and well deserved.

But for us to be worthy of the tag *dog's best friend*, we must endeavor to understand them as well as they understand us. In order to become the best possible friends for our dogs, we must first comprehend how they experience the world. A look into the canine brain and sensory system will show us how dogs capture and process information—essentially, how they think—and this will help us to better understand why they behave as they do. Fortunately, the gains of science over the past twenty years have allowed a great deal of insight into the inner workings of our canine best friends.

Canine Cognition

The study of canine cognition, which differs from the educational learning theory known as cognitivism, is a comparatively recent undertaking for scientists, and it is an especially complex endeavor for several reasons. The first reason is that arriving at an exact definition of *cognition* is no simple task. The general concept of cognition, what an individual does with information acquired from the outside world, is relatively easy to comprehend. It's when precise questions—such as *What types of information are acquired through what processes?*—are asked that the difficulties begin. The best definition I've been able to develop is that cognition refers to *the mental processes involved in comprehension, knowledge, and understanding, including but not limited to thought, memory, judgment, empathy, planning, and perception.*

The second limiting factor is that many different disciplines are seeking to understand cognition in dogs from their own individual perspectives, and they must consult and communicate with one another to prevent analysis bias. Among those studying canine cognition across various disciplines are evolutionary anthropologists such as Dr. Brian Hare, at the Duke Canine Cognition Center, neuroscientists like Dr. Gregory Berns, at Emory University, psychologists like Dr. Stanley Coren, at the University of British Columbia, and ethologists like Dr. Adam Miklosi, at the Family Dog Project in Budapest. Each scientific discipline has a slightly different focus and interpretative approach to the data.

The third complication is the difficulty in actually testing cognition in dogs, particularly in light of something known as the Clever Hans effect. In 1904, among the hottest celebrities in Germany, indeed in most of Europe, was a Russian trotting horse named Clever Hans. A retired German schoolteacher named Wilhelm von Osten had purchased Clever Hans four years prior. Mr. von Osten wanted to use his skills as an educator to prove animals capable of complex cognition, and based on Clever Hans's performance, he appeared wildly successful. Clever Hans, using his front right hoof, would paw the answers to amazingly complex math problems and shake his head to indicate *yes* and *no*.

Skeptics immediately suspected Mr. von Osten was somehow cueing Clever Hans as to the correct answers. However, Clever Hans could also answer questions posed by certain other people, some of them skeptics themselves, when Mr. von Osten wasn't present, so he clearly wasn't providing answers. Finally, a researcher realized three things that enabled him to figure out just how the horse was able to answer such difficult questions: Clever Hans could only answer questions posed by certain people with whom he had developed something of a connection; he had to be able to see his questioner in order to answer correctly; and the person asking the question had to know the answer himself. It turned out that Clever Hans was able to recognize signals so subtle as to be unrecognizable by the person giving them, and those signals allowed him to figure out the correct responses.

His fans were greatly disappointed. Though no ruse was apparently intended, those who believed the horse capable of such advanced thinking felt duped. Scientists took the saga as a serious warning that one must be extremely careful about attributing cognitive prowess to animals when in fact other factors could be at work. Everyone who has since studied cognition has been warned to avoid any chance of what became known as the Clever Hans effect. Rather than avoiding it, I think we should celebrate the Clever Hans effect for the remarkable ability that it represents.

From my perspective, Hans wasn't merely clever, he was a social genius. Imagine being able to recognize nonverbal signals so subtle as to be undetectable by the individual actually giving the cues. That is one powerful skill. Luckily for us, a single Russian trotting horse wasn't the only one who has ever had this ability. Our dogs have it too, and you will see in coming chapters how we can capitalize on this remarkable skill.

Nonetheless, Clever Hans taught scientists that there are many ways researchers can accidentally influence an animal's behavior, and extreme care must be taken to avoid manipulation. In research with dogs, there is also the potential for giving an accidental odor-based clue. For example, in an effort to test whether a dog understands that the pot marked by a yellow strip contains food, we must be sure that the dog cannot smell the food or that all the choices smell equally. Finally, there is the question of whether or not a dog is motivated to perform in studies. There is a significant difference between a dog *knowing* something and a dog *demonstrating that he knows* something. It seems likely that lack of motivation is the primary reason why dogs have not done well with the test most commonly used to indicate self-recognition, known as the mirror test.

In the 1970s, psychologist Gordon Gallup created an experiment designed to determine whether animals have the ability of self-recognition. In the assessment, an animal is surreptitiously marked with two dots of colored dye. The first dot is positioned so as to be visible to the animal when he is looking in the mirror. The second dot is invisible in the reflection. If the animal appears to react to the visible dot, such as by scratching, rubbing, or pawing at it, while at the same time not reacting at all to the nonvisible one, he is thought to have self-recognition. More simply stated, if he reacts to something he sees in the mirror and not to something he only *feels*, then he must have recognized the image in the mirror as himself. Human children begin to pass this test at approximately eighteen months of age. Conversely, dogs do not pass the mirror test at all.

But I find giving dogs the mirror test to be nonsensical. In order to react to the dot, dogs must see the dot and then care enough about it to be interested. Vision is not a dog's strongest asset, and I'm not sure that dogs care enough about marks on their body to react to that sort of visual stimulus. Perhaps a better test of self-recognition for dogs might somehow involve scent. My own dogs never feel the need to mark where they've urinated previously unless another dog has been there. This is compelling evidence that my dogs can recognize their own scent, and therefore are capable of self-recognition.

The Canine Brain

Picture both the human brain and the canine brain as a golf club, specifically a driver, inside its protective cover. The shaft of the club is the brain stem, or reptilian brain. The brain stem is responsible for survival functions, such as breathing, heart rate, metabolism, and sleep cycles. The head of the golf club is the limbic, or mammalian, brain, which is responsible for, among other things, emotion and memory. The protective cover is the neocortex, which controls higher cognitive functions, such as language, logic, planning, and creativity. When comparing human and canine brains, other than mere size, the primary difference is the neocortex. The human neocortex is proportionally much larger than that of a dog, allowing humans a greater capacity for advanced mental processes.

Vision

Contrary to popular belief, dogs are not completely color-blind. Rather, they are red-green color-blind, meaning that they can see blues and yellows. Recently, Russian scientists conducted an experiment to determine if dogs can use color to guide them in decision-making. They used light yellow, dark yellow, light blue, and dark blue markers to indicate which one of four otherwise identical boxes contained food. The dogs in their experiment were able to correctly identify the colored markers and, by doing so, select which airtight box contained the treat, a strong indication that color is at least somewhat important for dogs.

Visual acuity is measured by what is known as the Snellen

fraction, an assessment of what can be seen at a certain distance. Personally, I have horrible vision—without correction, 20/240, meaning that what the average person can see from a distance of 240 feet I cannot see until I'm 20 feet away. Most dogs have vision that is around 20/80, meaning the average person has visual acuity four times better than that of a dog. Humans have more cones, the retinal cells responsible for visual acuity, than dogs do.

While humans have more cones, dogs have more rods, retinal cells responsible for vision in low light and motion detection. So dogs have excellent night vision and can see motion far better than we can. Many predatory mammals have similar retinal structure, explaining why some prey animals freeze rather than run when confronted by a predator. If they are still, they might not be seen.

Dogs also have a slightly larger visual field than humans do, because their eyes are set on the sides of their head. However, their eye placement also means that they have a relatively small area of *binocular vision*, the type of vision in which both eyes see the same thing at the same time. Binocular vision is particularly important for judging distances, something dogs do not do as well as humans.

Also, most dogs are low to the ground relative to humans, so their visual field is obviously different. Logically, they are more familiar with our lower legs than our eyes. At Canine Assistants, we believe it's critically important for dogs to learn to look up at their human partner's face. Consequently, it is one of the first behaviors we encourage with our puppies.

Hearing

Most experts believe that dogs and humans can hear equally well in terms of volume and distance, though the average dog likely listens more intently and can make better use of sounds thanks to the unique shape and flexibility of their ears. Dogs can also hear at a much higher pitch. Pitch is determined by the frequency of sound waves; the more vibrations that occur in a second, the higher pitched the sound. Dogs can hear frequencies of 40,000 to 100,000 vibrations per second, whereas humans can hear only up to about 20,000 vibrations per second.

While high-pitched sounds, such as those made by dog whistles and anti-barking devices, catch most dogs' attention, they are painful. High-pitched, painful noises may be the reason many dogs are afraid of items with small motors, such as vacuum cleaners and ceiling fans. I'm never in favor of using force, intimidation, or pain with dogs, so I don't believe in using high-pitched noises to control them.

On the flip side, I am in favor of using soothing noises to help dogs. I met a wonderful woman named Lisa Spector and her amazing Lab, Sanchez, on my first book tour. Lisa is a concert pianist and one of the creators of *Through a Dog's Ear* music (there is also a book by the same name), designed to help dogs relax based on the principles of psychoacoustics, the study of sound perception. Lisa explained to me that sounds have a profound physiological effect. Complex sounds excite the nervous system, while sounds that are more easily interpreted by the brain, *simple sounds,* as Lisa calls them, are calming to the nervous system.

Lisa and her partner, Joshua Leeds, have developed the iCalm, an iPod-like device for dogs. All of our Canine Assistants dogs love listening to the iCalm, quickly falling asleep when it's turned on each evening. In addition to the relaxing music, the program also includes the Canine Noise Phobia Series, designed for dogs who have noise sensitivities.

Smell

It's been said that people live in a *world of vision*, while dogs live in a *world of smell*, so allow me to use a visual analogy to explain how truly powerful a dog's nose is. If dogs could see as well as they could smell, then what we can see at a distance of one-third of a mile, a dog could see equally well at a distance of three thousand miles. Put another way, most dogs can smell a single bad apple in a field of 2 million barrels. Dogs' noses are lined with approximately 300 million scent receptors compared to the 6 million found in the human nose. How fortunate we are that they are so willing to use this extraordinary ability for our benefit.

Recently, Brent Craven, a bioengineer at Penn State, led a team that discovered dogs actually split the air they inhale. From each breath, approximately 88 percent of the air is used for respiration, while the remaining 12 percent is used for scent collection. The portion used for scent collection is diverted to a small nook in the back of the nose where bony, scroll-shaped structures called turbinates sit. Lining the turbinates is tissue that recognizes odor molecules based on shape and electrical signature before sending the information on to the olfactory lobe in the brain for analysis. It is estimated that dogs use forty times more of their brain capacity for scent than humans do.

As if all of that weren't enough to turn dogs into scenting superheroes, they also have an additional scent detection apparatus, the vomeronasal organ, which humans lack altogether. The vomeronasal organ sits just above the roof of a dog's mouth and is used for the detection of pheromones, chemicals that provide social information, such as reproductive status, to members of the same species.

But pheromones aren't merely about reproduction. They also provide information about an individual's physical and psychological status. I suspect that dogs can scent-detect human pheromones and that is a large part of their ability to discern blood sugar changes, and maybe even impending seizures. We often see our service dogs making a teeth-chattering motion, pushing scent into their vomeronasal organ, when they alert to oncoming seizures.

Taste

Dogs have only 1,700 taste buds, in comparison to 9,000 in humans, but it seems that their incredible sense of smell significantly enhances their enjoyment of food. Among those 1,700 taste buds are receptors for sweet, salty, sour, savory, and bitter flavors. Unlike humans, dogs also have special receptors for water at the tip of the tongue. These receptors become more sensitive when a dog eats foods that are sweet or salty, times when the body might require additional fluids for optimal function.

Touch

Touch not only allows newborn puppies to determine where to get milk and how to stay close to Mom and littermates for warmth, it also facilitates bonding by producing oxytocin and other hormones associated with attachment. A study measuring oxytocin levels in dogs after separation from their people revealed that levels rise when your dog simply sees you, increasing even more when you speak to your dog. The highest and most lasting spike occurs when you touch your dog upon returning home. Dogs love the sight, sound, and smell of us, but it is our touch they crave. (Please see Appendix D on massage techniques for more information on using touch with your dog.)

Canine Emotion

Dr. Jaak Panksepp is a neuroscientist who coined the term *affective neuroscience* to refer to the neural mechanisms of emotion. Dr. Panksepp has done a tremendous amount of research on emotion in nonprimate animals, and he has identified seven core emotional systems that all animals experience, which he calls the blue-ribbon emotions. He always writes them in all capitals as homage to his belief, shared by Darwin, that emotional response is evolutionary in origin and fundamental to the survival of the individual and the species. The descriptions below pertain specifically to the way that dogs experience these emotions, but they are common to all mammals.

PANIC is experienced as the result of separation distress, loneliness, social loss, and grief. The need for social contact is hardwired into the canine brain, and even when not life threatening, the loss of valued social contact can be emotionally painful. Dogs are paedomorphic, meaning that they retain juvenile characteristics into adulthood. Perhaps this accounts, to some extent, for the separation anxiety that is common and often serious in dogs. While the effects can be highly distressing, with professional help, separation anxiety is treatable.

RAGE is the emotional system that gives one the feeling of frustration when one is being restrained or restricted in the face of danger. For dogs, leashes, fences, crates, and even the inside of a vehicle can elicit this response. Rage often results in behavior labeled as aggressive, including barking, snarling, and, in extreme cases, biting. The key to managing this emotion is to reduce the restraint or at least create the impression of doing so. One of the most valuable lessons my veterinarian husband taught me about restraining dogs for medical procedures is that a light hold is far more effective than a tight one.

SEEKING is the emotional system that gives one a feeling of pleasurable anticipation. For humans, the dopamine-driven seeking system is what helps us get out of bed each day. It's also what causes us to become addicted to the hunt for the largest trout or the perfect pair of shoes. In dogs, seeking is largely tied to the behaviors innate to the species as a whole, such as hunting or savaging, or to those common to specific breeds, such as retrieving for sporting dogs or working sheep for herders. When a dog follows your hand while you hold out a treat, that's seeking.

FEAR is the feeling of threat, foreboding, or pain, and it's typically followed by fighting, fleeing, or freezing, depending on the individual's evaluation of the circumstances. Though fear is necessary for survival, it causes universally unpleasant feelings, and long-term or frequent experience of fear can have harmful physical and emotional effects. Since dogs do not share our language, it is often difficult to communicate to them that fear in a particular circumstance is unfounded. It helps to remain calm ourselves, relaxing our bodies and speaking in a casual, matter-of-fact tone, allowing our dogs time to decide on their own that their fearfulness is unwarranted. Fortunately, as Dr. Panksepp reports, the fear and seeking systems cannot function simultaneously, so anything that can get dogs into seeking mode, such as tossing treats or squeaking a toy, should either prevent or bring them out of fear.

PLAY is the emotional system that controls behaviors done for the purpose of enjoyment. Play is so vital to mammals that the need for it is built into the brain. I've noticed that older dogs are often revitalized by the presence of playful puppies and energetic young adults, and I've seen the same response in people. So why does the attendance of youth have such a profound impact on mature adults across species lines? There are doubtless multiple components involved, but in large part, the answer is that the young stimulate the endorphin-rich play system. In any species, the importance of play for maintaining a positive state of mind cannot be overemphasized.

LUST is the system tied to reproductive behaviors. Reproduction, as a biological imperative, exerts tremendous influence over the thoughts, feelings, and actions of all species. Consequently, reproductive status must be taken into consideration when working with dogs. The influence of hormones and lust can be a highly nuanced issue, and it may be necessary to seek professional guidance from veterinarians or behaviorists when intact males or females are exhibiting related problem behaviors.

CARE is the nurturance system in mammals. Though often thought of exclusively as maternal, the care system is actually responsible for all nonsexual expressions of attachment. This system is obviously active in most dogs, evidenced by their affection and devotion toward those they love.

Though many pet parents believe that their dogs experience guilt, there is no evidence that this is true. In order for our dogs to feel guilty about doing something that we people perceive as wrong, they must have a clear understanding of our human code of conduct and an awareness of the precise actions they took that violated that code. That requires complex cognitive processes experts believe are beyond the range of dogs.

An experiment done by Dr. Alexandra Horowitz at Columbia University showed guilt to be a function of *owner belief*, not evidence of misdoing. In her study, owners were asked to leave the room after admonishing their dogs not to eat a treat. In some cases, the dogs were able to eat the treat, and in other cases, they were prevented from eating it. But Horowitz told some of the pet parents the opposite of what had actually happened. When people thought their dogs were guilty of eating the forbidden treat, they believed their dogs looked guilty, whether they had actually eaten it or not.

The Orienting Response

The *orienting response* (OR) is a reflexive response to novel stimuli such as motion or sound in an animal's environment. It is an innate reaction designed to help answer the question *What is that?* The OR triggers a brief moment of immobility—the animal freezes—while cognitive and emotional concerns, such as whether the unique stimulus heralds something beneficial or something dangerous, are addressed. Immobility may continue if the animal considers that the best approach for maintaining personal safety. *Playing possum* by faking death is an extreme example of a prolonged freeze response used by opossums when their OR indicates potential danger.

Reptiles and mammals both demonstrate the orienting response; however, the reptilian orienting pattern appears to be purely reflexive. In mammals, the initial OR is followed by a nonreflexive attention phase during which the individual *attends* to the novel response by looking, listening, sniffing, barking, and contemplating the circumstance. It's during the attention phase that an animal decides on the appropriate course of action, which in dogs may include fight, flight, freeze, or play.

In dogs, the orienting response serves as a kind of bridge between their sensory capacities, which make orientation possible, and their cognitive abilities, which enable them to formulate a conscious response.

Canine Social Cognition

Dogs are highly attuned social animals and their social genius is at the very core of my philosophy. Because of it, they are far better led through bonding than they ever could be through dominating. It often seems that our dogs can read our minds, understandable when you remember that dogs as a species have been studying humans for more than ten thousand years. Conversely, we have been studying them seriously for only the past twenty years. We have some catching up to do.

Canine social cognition is an exciting topic for animal behaviorists, who have been surprised to discover that dogs appear to surpass our closest genetic relatives, chimpanzees and bonobos, in many assessments of interspecies social cognition. Determining whether this superior social cognition is the result of evolutionary changes to the species (known as phylogenetics) or instead the result of experiences within the lives of the individuals tested is of major interest to all assistance-dog programs. Service dogs must meet certain criteria in order to be successful, including the ability to remain focused on their human partners even in highly distracting environments. If an eight-week-old puppy cannot focus his attention on his handler, does this mean he's unlikely to become a successful service dog? If *evolutionary changes* to the species as a whole are exclusively responsible for dogs' attentiveness to humans, then perhaps this puppy simply isn't cut out for service. Conversely, if *individual experiences* are of primary importance, then the puppy, if educated appropriately, has an excellent chance of success. The question, again, is one of nature versus nurture. At Canine Assistants, we believe that nature provides the pieces but nurture puts them together. For the distracted puppy in question, we would design an educational plan that would help him focus on the person who needs him.

The Canine Code of Conduct

Dogs, like all social species, live by a set of social rules, and the following Canine Code of Conduct helps us recognize and respect what is most important to them. These rules govern a dog's behavior as well as his interactions with other animals and people. Though some might seem obvious to seasoned dog parents, it never hurts to review them. If dogs could speak our language, here is how they might explain them to us:

"I would never do something merely to anger or frustrate you." This is the most important rule. By most estimates, domestic dogs first came into existence between ten thousand and thirty-five thousand years ago. Yet, in that time, they have rapidly integrated themselves into our lives and taken up residence around the globe. In sizes from tiny Chihuahuas to enormous Great Danes, the 400-million-plus dogs alive today are one of the most successful animal species on earth. Why? Because they know how to coexist with us and make us happy. Dogs need man in order to flourish, and their behavior reflects this need. Dogs have evolved to please us, so know that when your dog frustrates you, it isn't because he deliberately set out to do so.

"I know that you are in charge." The wonderful writer Anne Tyler once said, "Ever consider what they must think of us? I mean, here we come back from a grocery store with the most amazing haul—chicken, pork, half a cow. They must think we're the greatest hunters on earth!" Our dogs already know we are the leaders. We simply need to reassure them we will be good ones.

"Human isn't my native language." You cannot expect your dog to comply when you say, "Rover, do not eat that turkey on the kitchen counter, because it's for Thanksgiving dinner." While dogs are capable of learning many individual words, understanding our language doesn't come easily to them, so it's best to keep your expectations low when issuing verbal directives. In other words, your dog might leave you a drumstick, but I wouldn't count on it.

"If it's edible, I'll eat it." In a dog's mind, and based on his instincts, available food should either be eaten immediately or hidden for later consumption. Most dogs seem to live with the certainty that famine is just around the corner. Given that dogs appear to have come from a long line of hunters and scavengers, this makes a great deal of sense. Food makes life possible. When you are not the one who can operate the can opener or drive the car to the market, food becomes even more precious.

Given dogs' strong natural tendencies in this arena, it's little surprise that one of the most frequent questions I'm asked is how to keep dogs from eating things we don't want them to have.

There are three possible approaches, only two of which I can endorse as a solution:

- You can condition your dog to fear places you might leave food, such as kitchen counters, by using devices such as mousetraps and shock collars. The huge negative to this approach is that you might end up with a dog who is afraid in his own home, perhaps even afraid of you . . . a price that is far too high. This approach is to be avoided at all costs.

- Teach your dog that he should eat food only when you give him permission. This can be a lifesaver for dogs who perform search and rescue and other types of work where eating found food might be harmful. However, teaching this kind of automatic "Leave it" is difficult. It takes a great deal of time, much work, and absolute consistency on your part.

- Do not leave things you do not want your dog to eat, hide, or chew in areas that are accessible to him. This is the method I employ with my own dogs. It's simple and it works.

"Force is always my last resort." True aggression that causes significant injury is not something a dog wants to use. Dogs will do almost anything to avoid using their teeth to cause harm. Puppies first learn bite inhibition from their mothers and their littermates. The exception to this dictum is when dogs respond reflexively in self-defense to something that causes pain or fear, making rational thought impossible.

"If something is in my possession, it belongs to me." Possession is 100 percent of the law to dogs. Adult dogs will not take toys or bones away from even the smallest of pups. The only exception to this rule is occasionally seen with dogs in the same family, but tacit permission by the possessor is almost surely granted in these cases. Humans are the ones who insist on being able to take our dogs' possessions whenever we choose, and for the most part, they allow us to do so.

"Never invade the space of another without permission." This is a law of dogdom that is often violated by dogs who are not socially savvy, and the violation is quite likely to earn a stern correction. I frequently see this at dog parks, and often the dog who corrects the transgressor by snapping or snarling is the one reprimanded by the people present. These relatively polite snaps and snarls are actually a great kindness, since space invaders (dogs who haven't learned proper social skills) are at risk from dogs who might be more aggressive with their corrections. This is another dog law people break on a regular basis.

"I don't want to soil where I sleep or spend time." While dogs don't want to toilet where they spend time, they don't intuitively understand the concept of toileting exclusively outside the home. Areas of your house, such as guest rooms, where your dog doesn't spend much time should be blocked off when you are housebreaking. What we consider inappropriate soiling can occur when dogs are ill, stressed, have the need to mark certain areas, or simply cannot hold it. None of these circumstances represent deliberate *misbehavior* on the part of your dog, so it is best to ignore the accident, after cleaning the area with a product designed to eliminate pet odors, and focus on patiently addressing the underlying cause of the soiling.

Here are a few more important principals that our dogs live by:

- Bonding with those I love and care about is of primary importance.
- I forgive others quickly and completely.
- If it runs from me, I should chase it. If it chases me, I should run from it.
- I never approach someone head-on. That might be seen as threatening.
- If something scares me, I try to look larger. If it terrifies me, I try to look smaller.
- If it's human, I try extremely hard to make it happy.

Having an increased awareness of how dogs perceive and function in the world helps us better understand why they do what they do. It allows us to become as good friends to them as they've been to us from the beginning of our time together—for to know dogs is most certainly to love them.

Five

Dog Speak

The class for our volunteers and their foster dogs had run a little longer than anticipated. As I was summing up what we'd covered, I noticed that one young Lab had become antsy, wiggling constantly while his canine classmates were mostly dozing. Before I could suggest to his volunteer that her dog needed to go to the bathroom, the dog reached into the woman's supply bag, grabbed a roll of poop bags, and dropped them in her lap. Point made.

Not all communication between dogs and people is quite so clear. Yet communication is at the heart of every relationship. One of the most important roles we play in the lives of our dogs is that of interpreter, learning what their communicative signals mean as well as helping them understand ours. Fortunately, while we don't share the same language, we do seem to share some of the same communication skills.

Voice and Emotion

It turns out that dogs and people are remarkably similar in the way they process voice and emotion. Definitive evidence of this similarity was produced in a study led by Attila Andics, PhD, of Hungary's Eötvös Loránd University and published in the February 20, 2014, issue of *Current Biology*. The subjects, eleven canine and twenty-two human participants, were exposed to various sounds while being given functional MRIs. While in the MRI scanner, each participant listened to nearly two hundred recordings of dog and human sounds, including whining, crying, laughing, and barking. The results revealed that both species had particular areas of the brain that showed increased blood flow when hearing vocalizations, particularly from their own species, and both showed similar changes in response to the emotional tone of the vocalization. Earlier studies discovered that *positive* vocalizations in humans and dogs tend to be higher pitched and shorter in duration than the longer, deeper sounds that convey *negative* emotions. It makes sense that dogs can recognize the emotion behind our words far more easily than precise meaning.

Dogs and Language

While dogs can (and do) learn words in our language, this does not appear to be a particularly easy task for them. For this reason, spoken language can be confusing to dogs when they are initially developing a relationship with a human. With a little work, however, dogs may be able to develop a far larger vocabulary of human words than we previously believed possible. Psychologist John Pilley has taught his border collie, Chaser, more than a thousand names for toys and items, as well as a handful of verbs such as *paw, nose,* and *take,* allowing him to interact with those items in multiple ways. Chaser shows clear evidence of dogs' ability to *fast map* (to learn new concepts from just one exposure) and use inferential reasoning by exclusion. While border collies are known to be highly intelligent, there is nothing that indicates that all dogs couldn't learn just as many words as Chaser if someone had the time and patience to teach them.

The research that we've done at Canine Assistants indicates that dogs who are securely attached to a person and taught using Bond-Based Choice Teaching appear to learn the meaning of words, both spoken and written, far more quickly than those trained with traditional positive reinforcement. We taught four eight-month-old puppies who had been trained using positive reinforcement and four eight-month-old puppies who had been taught using only Bond-Based Choice Teaching to match three objects (a pen, a glove, and a wallet) to both the spoken words and the written words for the objects. It took twenty-six repetitions on average for the positive reinforcement group to learn to match the objects with the spoken and written words, while it took the Bond-Based dogs only eight repetitions. There are several possible reasons for this result, including the fact that the positive reinforcement dogs appeared to be more focused on obtaining the reward for making the correct choice than on understanding the task. The positive reinforcement dogs also appeared more concerned about the potential of making the wrong choice, thereby not receiving the food reward and the praise of their handler, which limited their opportunities to learn from mistakes. In any case, we are continuing to test the difference that teaching methods appear to have on the receptive communication skills of our dogs.

In addition to being able to learn *receptive* communication skills—the skills involved in understanding what others are trying to convey to them—dogs excel in productive communication, that is, in expressing themselves to others. For a long time, scientists believed that most barking was meaningless. However, recent research indicates that barking might have more meaning than initially thought. Dogs have what is known as a reasonably *modifiable vocal tract*, making it possible for them to deliberately produce a variety of sounds that vary in pitch, tone, amplitude, and timing. These different sounds likely have different meanings that are easily recognizable to other dogs.

Dogs also use their voices with remarkable effectiveness. And for the most part, we understand what our dogs are saying or, at least, how they are feeling. A study done by Péter Pongrácz, PhD, of Eötvös Loránd University in Hungary, and published in the *Journal of Comparative Psychology* in May 2005, found that most people could tell whether a dog was being aggressive, fearful, or playful based solely on an audio recording. (If you are interested in knowing more about the meaning of your dog's vocalizations, please see the Dictionary of Dog Sounds in Appendix E.)

Canine Body Language

While dogs can be very vocal, they communicate primarily by using body language. Much consternation and heartache could be avoided if we were able to understand what dogs are trying to say, but the body language of dogs can be challenging to decipher. Below, I have given you some of the spots to watch when trying to understand what your dog's body is saying.

CANINE BODY LANGUAGE SPOTS TO WATCH:

Overall Body: Tight muscles indicate some form of tension. A stiff, frozen posture often indicates that a dog is feeling threatened and is considering the appropriate action. Contracted muscles usually mean that a dog is fearful or experiencing pain. Conversely, relaxed muscles mean a relaxed dog.

Tail: As most people know, a tail that is tucked or tightly clinched indicates fear. What many people do not realize is that a wagging tail doesn't always mean a happy, approachable dog. As a matter of fact, a tail that is wagging with little side-to-side motion often indicates anxiety or irritation. When a dog is happy, he will wag his tail farther to the left than right, while an anxious dog wags farther to the right than the left.

Ears: Ears held tightly against the skull or farther back than their normal position are indicative of a worried or annoyed dog. Ears that are perked up beyond their normal set show that the dog is interested in something. For a dog who has floppy ears, holding one ear lower than the other is often the first noticeable sign of an earache.

Mouth: The corners of the mouth are called the commissures. When a dog is worried, the commissures of his mouth are often noticeably drawn down or up in a smiling, appeasing expression. A dog who is angry will show tightly clamped lips or an open mouth with commissures tight enough to bounce a quarter off of. A happy, relaxed dog has commissures that are loose and free of tension.

Following Referential and Ostensive Signals

What cognitive mechanisms are behind the social genius of dogs? We've known since the 1998 studies done by the Family Dog Project and Max Planck Institute that dogs appear to be the only species other than humans that can follow our *referential signals*, such as pointing and eye gazes. Dogs trust our signals so strongly that they will often make maladaptive choices, such as going to a cup they know to be empty rather than to one full of treats merely because a human points or looks toward the empty cup. However, it's only recently that scientists have been able to produce strong evidence that dogs can understand *ostensive signals* as well as referential ones. Ostensive signals *precede* a communication and include vocalizations, eye contact, gestures, or touch directed toward others to emphasize that *the information to follow* pertains to them.

The difference between referential and ostensive is subtle, so let's use an example. When a physician glances at his instrument tray, indicating to a nurse what he needs, this is a referential signal. But it was an ostensive signal when his eyes made contact with her first, indicating that he was about to give her important information. Knowing that dogs have the ability to understand both ostensive and referential signals is extremely important. Dogs are not merely capable of hearing us; they are capable of understanding that we *want* them to listen.

In 2012, psychologist Erno Téglás, PhD, of Central European University, devised a study to learn more about ostensive communication in dogs. Dr. Téglás adapted equipment designed to track eye movement, previously employed on preverbal human children, to be used on sixteen dogs he'd selected for the study. The dogs were placed, one at a time, in front of a large video screen, on which a young woman was visible in the center. To her left and right were identical box-like containers. In the ostensive communication trial, the young woman would look directly at the dog and say "Hello" in a happy, high-pitched tone. Then, she would turn her gaze toward one of the two containers. However, in the non-ostensive trial, the young woman did not look at the dog first, and she said "Hello" in a much less engaging manner, though, as before, she turned her head toward one of the containers. The dogs stared considerably longer at the container in the ostensive trial, evidence that they understood the communication was directed at them.

Understanding the Perspective of Others

When dogs respond to human signals, no matter what form they take, it is known as *receptive communication,* but this is only one category of canine social cognition. Another is *perspective taking,* which refers to dogs' ability to understand that others can have different perspectives from their own. Multiple studies have shown that dogs are more likely to disobey the cue "Leave it" if their humans have their eyes closed or if it's dark in the room, meaning they realize they can see the cookie but the person cannot. Other research has demonstrated that dogs will position themselves in front of a person to solicit attention and that they are more likely to follow the instructions of someone directly facing them, all evidence that they are aware of the states of others.

Recently, additional studies have provided evidence that dogs are able to understand that sometimes they have information that others do not. This phenomenon is displayed at Canine Assistants each time our new service-dog teams take their practical examination prior to graduation. One of the evaluations involves removing the human partner from the room as the canine partner watches someone hide a highly desirable object, such as a piece of rawhide, in a place that is out of the reach of the dog. When the human partner returns, 90 percent of the time, the dog's initial movement is to show his partner where the object is hidden, indicating that the dog realizes his human needs help finding the bone. The ability to understand what someone else knows and does not know is a critical part of social cognition and communication.

Changing Our Vocabulary to Help Our Dogs Build Theirs

One of the first things I learned about dog training was that you never asked a dog to do something; you told him. But now I understand that our desire to control dogs by telling them what to do is undermining their ability to control themselves. *Telling* a dog what to do means he doesn't have to think, and when circumstances arise that require thought—when you're not there, for example—the dog is panicked, thus reducing his self-confidence. Conversely, *asking* a dog to do something allows him to cognitively process the request and formulate an appropriate response, thus permitting him a sense of self-determination and increasing his confidence. *Asking* also invokes collaboration and enhances your bond. In accordance with our philosophy of collaborating with our dogs, we need to stop using the term *cue*. *Cue*, in the dog world, has lost the original meaning of "prompt," and has become virtually synonymous with command. Why not simply use the word that exactly matches our intention—*ask*.

It might seem as if asking would be less effective than using formal cues or commands. But let's remember the important influence of the dog-human bond. Simply stated, a strong bond gives dogs the motivation to behave in ways that will please us. So if the bond is there, when you ask, your dog will say *yes* if at all possible.

Communicating Our Asks

While our goal is to have dogs use social information to direct their own behavior, there will always be times when we must directly ask our dogs to do something for or with us. The easiest way to accomplish this is to teach our dogs the meaning of certain words. When teaching dogs language, think of splitting things up into *verbs*, those *asks* that involve a change in demeanor or position, and *nouns*, the labels we use to denote certain individuals, places, and things. Because dogs are learning new words and associations in what is to them a very foreign language, we must remember to be extremely patient.

ACTION WORDS

The action words we want to teach dogs fall into several categories. Here are the groupings and words I use:

Demeanor Changes

Playtime means being wildly excited and playful.

Settle means calming down.

Patience means waiting quietly for a moment or two.

Relax means settling down for an extended period of time.

Gentle means being careful when using your mouth or paws.

Combination Demeanor and Action Changes

Visit means placing your chin in someone's hand or lap.

Easy means walking slowly and without pulling on the leash.

Freeze means being still and letting someone come to you.

Position Changes or Actions

Touch means lightly pressing your nose into a designated spot.

Come means moving closer to someone.

Go means moving away from someone.

Better hurry means eliminate now.

Watch means focus on someone.

Trade means giving someone what you have and getting something in return even if it's just a simple "Thank you" or a scratch on the chest.

NOUNS AND LABELS

Teach your dogs labels for common objects, places, or individuals, including:

His or her name

Your name

Names of others in your household

Name of his safe zone, such as his bed or cubby

Names of his favorite toys

Teaching Your Dog His Vocabulary Words

The best learning sessions are short ones, so plan on working for only five to ten minutes at a time before taking a play or rest break. As soon as your dog's enthusiasm seems to be waning, stop for the day. Learning needs to be *fun*! I enjoy doing quick sessions of only a minute or two with our dogs many times a day.

Each time, before beginning vocabulary work with your dog, help him get comfortable by using this *food sharing* exercise, similar to the one I described earlier with Chase and the anxious golden, Bess. Find a small piece of food, such as a cracker or half slice of cheese that is both safe and palatable to you and your dog. Break off and eat a tiny piece of the food item yourself, then break off another small piece for your dog. Encourage your dog as he shares the food with you by saying whatever feels right, such as "What a good dog," in a happy, upbeat way. Add a good scratch or rub to your kind words whenever possible. Giving your dog food in this way may go against everything you've heard about training techniques, but I'm asking you to trust me. Sharing food with your dog in this context is a form of social bonding, and it will increase his trust in and attention to you.

Most of the verbs above can be taught by demonstrating the meaning for your dog and asking him to replicate your behavior.

TOUCH: Begin by cutting a small piece of brightly colored (preferably blue or yellow) duct or electrical tape and placing it on the back of your hand. Then extend your hand toward your dog with your palm facing inward. When your dog sniffs the tape on your hand, very lightly press the tape on his nose, saying "Touch" as you do so. Note his success in a big way, saying "Yay you! Good Touch!" If your dog doesn't sniff, rub a bit of good-smelling food on the tape to encourage him. But be careful to wipe off any solid pieces so he doesn't lick the tape instead of merely sniffing it. If he still does not understand the request, touch your nose briefly to the tape as you say "Touch," marking your success by saying something like "Yay me! Good Touch!" before extending your hand toward your dog again.

Touch is the basis for many behaviors, so be certain your dog learns it clearly by moving your hand into different positions and then transferring the piece of target tape onto a wall, chair, or other surface at nose height for your dog.

PLAYTIME: Let yourself go wild. Jump up and down, spin, dance, or dash from side to side, saying "Playtime!" excitedly. As your dog starts to get playful, note his success with "Yay you!"

SETTLE: After demonstrating excitement for a moment, suddenly relax your body and be still. As you calm down, lightly cup your hand on the side of your dog's face and ask him to calm down by saying "Will you settle" in a soothing voice. Your gentle touch on the side of your dog's face will act as a physical prompt to synchronize with you by calming down.

PATIENCE: *Patience* can easily be taught by pausing yourself before taking certain actions, such as crossing all indoor-to-outdoor thresholds. With your dog by your side on leash, pause before going through a doorway while saying "Patience." You can also teach the meaning of patience by asking your dog to pause for a moment before eating or chasing a ball. Be prepared to physically block access to his bowl or ball until he knows what patience means. The social component of this works best if you make the same action following being patient as your dog does, so try to set up learning situations where you can eat when he eats or run after the ball when he does.

RELAX: *Relax* means for the next short while nothing exciting is likely to happen and nothing will be expected of you, so consider this an excellent time to rest. This is best taught, like many *asks*, through synchronization with you. Sit or lie down in a quiet place where you and your dog can indeed rest safely for a few moments, then take a deep, noisy breath and exhale slowly. Relax your muscles and close your eyes while saying "Relax" in the most Zen-like voice possible, drawing out the syllables in a lazy way. Although you can open your eyes again, keep your lids feeling heavy and do not look directly at your dog. When your dog relaxes (whether in a sitting or down position), take another deep, sighing breath and quietly note his success. Be patient— dogs unaccustomed to this exercise may initially be a bit unnerved and find it difficult to relax, but all dogs will eventually lie down. Once you are relaxed together, remain so for at least two minutes.

GENTLE: My favorite way to begin teaching this word is by putting some form of mush-like, sticky food, such as a dab of peanut butter or squirt cheese, in the palm of my hand so that my dog has to lick at the substance rather than bite it. As the dog licks, say "Gentle" in a soft, slow manner, matching the tone of the word with the concept. Note his success with praise. After the lickable item is gone, put a piece of kibble in the palm of your hand and say "Can you be Gentle" in the same tone as you extend your hand toward your dog. It's fine if the dog uses his teeth to take the kibble (since we aren't teaching *Lick*), provided he does it gently. Note his success with praise. Next repeat the exercise with kibble placed between your thumb and forefinger. Note his success with praise.

VISIT: Place the tape you've been using to mark your Touch spot in one palm. Put your other hand, palm up, in front of the hand with the tape. Ask your dog to Touch the tape spot and position your other hand so that his chin is resting in your palm as he touches it. As he is touching, say "Will you Visit" and encourage him to leave his chin in your palm by gently massaging the side of his face with your fingers. Note his success with a quiet "Yay you!" This is a wonderful exercise for increasing your bond, so practice it often.

EASY: There are few things more difficult or less pleasurable than trying to take a casual walk with a large dog who pulls constantly on his leash. The good news is that it isn't difficult to teach your dog the meaning of the word *Easy*, and once you do, you can expect your walks together to be enjoyable. An excellent method is to say "Easy" as you begin walking together, then note his success enthusiastically before he can reach the end of the leash. Repeat the process until he begins to understand the word. If he pulls on you before you can note his success, just stop and stay as still as possible until he comes back toward you, releasing the tension on the leash. As soon as the leash goes slack, note his success enthusiastically.

COME and GO: If your dog knows the word *Touch*, then it's relatively simple to help him understand the meaning of the words *Come* and *Go*. Put a large, easily visible spot of the colored tape you've been using as your Touch target on a wall, chair, or similar object a few feet away, and another on your palm. Keeping your palm facing away from your dog so he does not see the tape on your hand, point at the other tape spot a few feet away and say, "Can you Go Touch." Note his success as he touches the tape. If he doesn't seem to understand your request, ask him to *Watch* as you demonstrate the task. Then, showing him your palm, say, "Will you come Touch," noting his success as he noses your palm. Once your dog has mastered this exercise, you can begin using *Go* whenever you want him to move away from you, such as when you throw a toy for him to retrieve, and *Come* whenever you want him to return to you.

FREEZE: You will need another person for this one. And bear in mind that we don't use *Freeze* in the form of a question as we do with other asks, since we want it to be a sharp startling vocalization. Begin with your dog on leash in a safely enclosed area (you will take him off leash quickly). As you and your dog are walking, have your helper suddenly call out "Freeze." Come to a complete stop when you hear "Freeze" and remain still and quiet until your helper, who should be walking quickly, approaches you and your dog and places a hand on each of you. After your helper's hand has made contact for a second or two, you can say, "Good Freeze! All done!" releasing him from position. Once your dog is freezing easily when he hears the word, take him off leash and continue practicing. After a few sessions with your helper, thank him or her and go it alone. First, walk with your dog on leash and come to a halt when you say "Freeze." Then put your hand on your dog for a long count of two before removing it, praising your dog, and starting to move again. Slowly increase the distance between you and your dog until you are successful from about fifty yards or so. Your dog will have to learn that it is okay for you to move but not for him to move, so take this part slowly.

BETTER HURRY: Take your dog on leash to a spot he often uses to potty and say to him, "Better hurry!" Increase your chances of success by taking him out at times when it is likely he will have to go, such as first thing in the morning. I find that it helps to let him sniff for a minute or so and then stay still so he can move around only a limited amount. This diminished area for sniffing seems to speed the process. Note his success with "Yay you!," but do it calmly so that you do not startle him mid-stream!

WATCH: There are many ways to teach your dog that *Watch* means please pay attention, and you may need to use multiple methods to help him grasp the concept. One of my favorite techniques is to place two plastic cups upside down on the floor, slipping a treat under one as you say "Would you please Watch?" Then move the cups around a bit before allowing him to find the treat. Note his success as you are moving the cups *before* he finds the treat (since Watch is what you're teaching, not finding the treat). Another method is to say "Can you Watch?" as you toss his favorite toy into one of several boxes you've arranged on the floor. Again, mark his success as he watches you toss the toy rather than when he finds it. You can also say "Would you please Watch?" as you move an object in your hand back and forth, marking his success as his eyes follow your movements.

TRADE: Since one of the primary rules in the Canine Code of Conduct is that it's wrong to take something away from someone else until they invite you do to so, it is always better to offer a trade when your dog has something you'd like to get, otherwise you risk being unacceptably rude. Teach the meaning of this word by saying "Want to Trade?" when your dog has a toy or ball and showing him the item you wish to give him in exchange. Note his success when he releases the item in his possession and takes whatever you've offered in swap. Initially, offer something of equal or greater value in your dog's mind, for example a treat. As your dog begins to understand the meaning of the word, your Trade offers can become slightly less enticing, such as an exuberant "Thank you" combined with a scratch on the chest.

HIS NAME: Say your dog's name in an upbeat tone. You can add a kissing noise or other sound to capture his attention if needed. When your dog looks at you, note his success. Remember, your dog's name should always sound safe and positive when coming from you, so never say it in anger or frustration.

NAMES OF OTHER INDIVIDUALS, PLACES, AND OBJECTS: You can teach your dog the names of other people, places, and items quite easily by using the verb *Touch*. Simply move a piece of the tape you have been using as your Touch spot to the individual, place, or object whose name you are teaching. For example, say you are teaching your dog that someone's name is Adam. With Adam standing close to your dog, put your tape on Adam's arm or leg and say, "Would you please Touch Adam?" When your dog puts his nose on the tape, note his success. Repeat by stationing Adam at increasing distances from your dog and asking your dog "Can you go Touch Adam?" Remember to note his success—your dog just learned the meaning of an entire sentence!

There are countless other nouns and verbs you can teach your dog, but keep in mind that the larger purpose in expanding your dog's vocabulary is less about teaching him the behaviors that accompany Touch, Gentle, Ick, or any explicit task and more about helping him understand the meaning of the words, which in turn enhances the level of communication between you. Use these vocabulary words when you need to communicate a specific request, and use these requests sparingly. As I mentioned at the start of the book, at Canine Assistants we do not let our recipients ask their dogs to do anything for the first week of recipient camp. We want them to focus on *bonding* with their dogs, not *bossing* them.

Giving your dog the skills and the opportunity to choose the appropriate way to act in any given situation without any direction from you is incredibly effective. Dogs have great memories and you may be astonished to see how easily prompted a dog is by his past behavior. When bonded, dogs have an intense desire to emulate you, and may very well copy your demeanor and behavior with no verbal request. Dogs also have high emotional intelligence, easily reading the emotions of others, and can thus be prompted, especially in terms of demeanor, merely by context.

While it's important to teach your dog certain words of human language so that the two of you can better communicate, it is equally (if not more) important for you to give your dog a chance to show how often asks are unnecessary. Great instructors know it is their job to prepare their students to function without them. A few years ago at Canine Assistants, I overheard one of my all-time favorite recipients talking to his dog. He didn't realize I was listening outside the room where they were standing, and I heard him say, "It won't take long, I promise, and after we finish we can go get a treat if you feel like it. I know you want to leave, buddy, but you just can't right now. You have to see Dr. Kent and get your shots." As I stood there, I could tell that though the dog didn't answer in human, he did answer, and the man gave words in his own mind to the dog's response. This man-dog team had always functioned beautifully together, and I realized I'd just accidentally eavesdropped on a big part of the reason why they did.

Give your dog a voice. It's okay if you misinterpret on occasion. The act of reciprocal communication is generally more valuable than the meaning therein. In other words, trying to understand your dog is usually all it takes.

Over the years, I've realized that dogs need the people they trust to understand their productive communication in order to feel secure. For example, if your dog urgently needs to relieve himself, I'm sure you understand his signals. Without two-way communication, a relationship is no more than a dictatorship, and while dogs can survive in a dictatorship, it's not the quality of life they deserve. For our service-dogs-in-training at Canine Assistants, productive communication can be remarkably challenging. While each of the dogs has a foster parent, a volunteer dedicated to that particular dog's development, all our dogs must also work with many other people during their time with us. It can be difficult for the dogs to make themselves clearly understood to multiple people.

To illustrate the importance of productive communication with our dogs, let's take the story of Moose, a golden retriever who was donated to Canine Assistants at three months of age. Although he was very well treated in his birth home and did not have any ingrained mistrust of people, he definitely didn't have total confidence in the directions of his human handlers. We work hard to instill an especially high level of trust in people in all our puppies from the day they are born, and Moose had some catching up to do in this regard.

Unfortunately, we made the mistake of insisting that Moose take a bath like our other puppies when he was clearly not comfortable with it. For Moose, the fear wasn't about bathing; it was about getting into the tub. It scared him, yet we made him do it. I'm convinced that there are two keys to helping dogs choose to do something we want them to do: time and distance. Dogs need the time to assess situations for themselves, at a distance from which they feel secure.

We did not give Moose either. Over a short period, he progressed from not wanting to get into the tub to not wanting to get into a car and then, at certain periods, to not wanting to move at all. In addition, his entire demeanor changed from exuberantly happy to depressingly sad. He'd reached the point where his behavior was jeopardizing not only his chances of being placed as a service dog, but his chances of living comfortably with people at all. We knew that Moose needed a way to communicate with us.

The best way to begin working with your dog on developing his voice is to teach him what *yes* and *no* mean. We taught Moose to say "Yes please" and "No thank you" by using two voice-recordable buttons that he could push with his nose. On one, I recorded "Yes please," and on the other, "No thank you." And we taught Moose to use them by simply making whatever he said yes or no to happen or not happen when he hit the corresponding button. We started with easy questions like "Do you want a treat?" From there, we moved on to "Do you want water?" or "Do you want to go outside?"

These simple devices made a huge difference almost immediately. We began by asking if he wanted to go for a ride or get a treat or take a bath. His answers were consistently "Yes please," "Yes please," and "No thank you," in that order. Somehow those two buttons, and our response to them, allowed Moose to trust us again. He still doesn't care for the bathtub, but he is an avid shower taker, something we discovered when we became desperate to find some way to get him clean while honoring his request to not have to get into the tub! Interestingly enough, Moose walked right into the shower stall without any prompting at all from us.

Teaching your dog to indicate yes and no is a simple process that can have a transformative effect on your relationship.

TEACHING YOUR DOG *YES* AND *NO*

Start by placing a yummy bit of food so that your dog can see it but not touch it. Rub your left palm on the food, being careful not to touch it with your right hand.

Ask your dog if he wants a treat (or whatever word you use for *treat*) while pointing and looking at the food.

Say "Yes?" while extending your left palm and "No?" while extending your right palm.[1]

When he sniffs (or paws at) the food smell on your left palm, say "Yes—okay" and hand him the treat.

Once he understands that touching your left palm means he is going to get the food, you can start adding other items and opportunities (such as going outside) to the mix. You can also use your hands to ask him other two-option questions, such as "Frisbee or ball?"

[1] If you like, you may switch your *yes* and *no* hands so that he realizes it is the word that is important rather than the hand, once he understands the idea of indicating a preference with his nose or paw.

Six

Canine Coursework

We use the word *teach* rather than *train* to denote help-ing our dogs learn the skills and behaviors they need to be successful in life. Why be so specific about the terms we are using? Subtle differences in vocabulary can make a big differ-ence in the way we feel about something, and this in turn can affect the way we interact with our dogs. At Canine Assistants, we believe that *train* suggests something we do *to* dogs, while *teach* suggests something we do *with* dogs, preparing them for life in such a way as to give them independence and agency. A simple change in our vocabulary makes a tremendous difference in how we relate to our dogs.

In order to effectively teach our dogs, we must start by decid-ing what skills our dogs need to learn.

Does *Sit* Really Mean Sit?

I once attended a conference during which the definition for the word *sit*, as it relates to a dog's behavior, was debated ad nauseam. My favorite suggestion came from a trainer friend from California: "Sit means please stop running around like a lunatic and act as if you have some manners, thereby making me feel like a good dog parent who has control over your behavior rather than a total slacker." While the final definition settled on at the conference was "placing one's haunches on the substrata," I saw a great deal of truth in my friend's submission.

When we ask our dogs to sit, what we really want is for them to be still and calm for a moment. Likewise, when we ask a dog to Lie Down, what we actually mean is be calm, quiet, and still for an extended period of time. This can be confusing for dogs who've been taught that cues are associated with certain movements of their bodies. And it can be confusing for people as well, when we watch our dog execute a perfect Lie Down, only to jump back up again a few seconds later.

Kevin, an instructor at Canine Assistants, told me a story that perfectly illustrates the problem with trying to control a dog's behavior with requests-for-action, such as Sit. He went to visit a friend whose dog, a wonderful yellow Lab, immediately jumped up on Kevin and began licking his face when he entered the friend's house. Kevin's embarrassed friend apologized, saying, "He isn't finished learning all his commands yet." But Kevin had loved the dog's playful greeting, and thought no apology was necessary.

Since there is no command routinely taught for Be less exuberant in your greeting, Kevin's friend was destined to be disappointed. Modern training teaches dogs to perform certain actions when so cued. Period. Yes, this man could train his dog to Sit and offer a paw to Shake when someone comes in the door, but eventually the dog is going to get up. Unless the man plans to be there to cue him twenty-four hours a day, seven days a week, his dog will ultimately be responsible for his own actions. What we really need, instead of external cues, is to teach our dogs what constitutes appropriate behavior in particular situations. This appropriate behavior can result in a change of physical position, such as going from a stand to a sit, but in many cases the actual behavioral change needs to be based in a change in your dog's excitement level—in other words, his *demeanor*. Your rules for appropriate canine demeanor can be anything you'd like, provided those rules are fair to your dog and good for the bond between you.

Educating Your Dog

Our job, in educating our dogs, is to be certain that they are Ready, Willing, and Able to be the best dogs possible.

> READY means they have the cognitive skill to determine what constitutes appropriate behavior at any given time.
> WILLING means they have the social and emotional skill to behave appropriately.
> ABLE means they are physically capable of behaving appropriately.

I've categorized exercises we can use to facilitate our dogs' overall education into three primary developmental domains:

1. *Cognitive Development Exercises:* These help your dog develop memory, behavior inhibition, discrimination, conceptual awareness, inferential reasoning, and productive and receptive communication.
2. *Socio-Emotional Development Exercises:* These build bonding, trust, self-reliance, confidence, social competence, deference, attentiveness, and motivation.

3. *Physical Development Exercises:* These focus on sensory awareness, gross motor skills, fine motor skills, fitness, and body awareness.

The educational exercises that follow are designed to strengthen your dog's abilities in each of these three categories, and you should be able to practice all of them at home. Your dog does not need to have any special skills or know any behaviors on signal in order to do these exercises. They are equally suitable for puppies and adult dogs.

Equipment Needed

Multiple cardboard boxes of various sizes and shapes

Pieces of low-value treat (like kibble)

Pieces of moderate-value treat (like Milk-Bone's soft and chewy treats)

Pieces of high-value treat (extremely tasty things given to your dog only on special occasions, like hot dogs or cheese)

Leash and collar

Two opaque plastic cups

A Hula-Hoop

Two toys your dog has never seen

One or two of your dog's favorite toys

Colored construction paper

Inexpensive dog toys that make strange noises, have strange textures, or are oddly shaped

A helper—optional but nice to have

Cognitive Development Exercises

Memory Development

EXERCISE 1: Take your dog for a short walk. While you're on your way out of the house, "hide" a few treats (or several of your dog's favorite toys), letting your dog see where you put the items, but not allowing him to access them. After returning home, as you near the items you've dropped, ask your dog, "Where are the treats?"

EXERCISE 2: With your dog in another room, put three pieces of different colored construction paper (yellows, blues, and whites are good choices) or something similar on the floor, each approximately four feet from the other. Label them *first, second,* and *third* in your mind. The papers do not have to be in any sort of line, simply well apart from one another. Then bring your dog into the room on leash and walk with him past each item in order, saying "First," then "Second," then "Third" as you pass them. Once you go by the third, say "Yes, that's it!" and make a huge fuss over how brilliant he is. Repeat the same exact pattern three or four times. Then allow your dog to leave the room for a play break of no more than three minutes. Return with your dog off leash and ask "Where first?" If he runs to the correct color, say "Yes, good dog," and ask "Where second?" and so on, until he takes you to all three spots. If he does not go to the correct color, say nothing but reattach his leash and walk the pattern several more times.

Be patient with both of these exercises. Some dogs seem to comprehend what you are asking immediately, and others take days to learn what you want. Few dogs are accustomed to taking charge by using their own memories to make decisions, and doing so can be a little unsettling for them at first. Remember though, *control* equals *confidence* equals *good mental health*.

Behavior Inhibition Development

EXERCISE 1: Practice going from indoors to outdoors with your dog and encouraging him to wait at every threshold he crosses, for at least a couple of seconds. Begin by saying "Patience" and blocking the doorway with your body, but little by little allow him to make the decision to wait even when the opening is available. Once your dog has learned to wait patiently for a few seconds, tell him how wonderful he is and encourage him to cross the threshold. This skill is critical for dogs. It helps them develop self-restraint and may one day keep them from bolting out the front door and into the street.

EXERCISE 2: Feeding your dog kibble by hand one piece at a time is a wonderful way to help him learn to inhibit his natural instinct to grab at food when it is in sight. It also helps him learn to be gentle when he gets his teeth near human skin. Hold a piece of kibble between your thumb and index finger so that your dog can see it. Then offer him the kibble, saying "Gentle" in a drawn-out manner as you let him sniff and nibble at the food. Always use words in a way that reflects the action they represent, so a request to be gentle should be said in a relaxed and calm manner. When your dog gently takes and chews the kibble, tell him how wonderful he is. If he is too rough, say "Uh-oh" and turn your fingers toward your body so that the back of your hand is in your dog's face. You want him to begin to understand that if he is rough, the food goes away. Your definition of *too rough* should become increasingly more demanding as your dog gets better at being gentle.

Once your dog is successful at taking kibble gently, repeat the exercise with a treat your dog especially loves, such as a small piece of bacon.

EXERCISE 3: While playing tug, fetch, or chase with your dog, suddenly call "Red light!" and stop moving completely. Your dog will continue to move first, but that's okay. After a count of five, say "Green light!" and begin playing again. Soon your dog will learn to stop when you say "Red light!" and when this happens, be sure to verbally praise him (with a low, soothing tone that doesn't make him want to move) for being so brilliant.

Learning Discrimination

Designate a particular toy with which your dog can play roughly. Let's call it the *rough toy*. This toy can be tugged, shaken, thrown, or whatever else your dog wants to do with it. Then replace that toy with another. This second toy, the *gentle toy*, is one with which your dog must be exceedingly gentle. It should be used only for this specific exercise, so be certain to keep it safely out of your dog's reach when you're not using it. Alternate between playing roughly with the *rough toy* and being calm and cautious with the *gentle toy* for about twenty to thirty seconds each. Play this game at least three or four days a week until your dog is proficient at following your verbal request that he be gentle. Remember to put these toys away when you are not playing with your dog.

Object Permanence

Turn a big cardboard box on its side to form a barrier. Have a helper hold your dog or, if you don't have a helper, safely secure your dog to a stationary object with his leash so he can watch you but not reach you. Show your dog a toy (or treat) and then place it behind the cardboard box out of his view. Take him off leash and ask him, "Where's your toy?" Slowly increase the difficulty of this exercise by using multiple boxes and moving the target item from one spot to another.

Inferential Reasoning by Exclusion

Get two twenty-ounce opaque plastic cups or two similar containers. With someone holding your dog (or his leash restraining him) so that he cannot reach but can watch you, turn the cups upside down on the floor and put a piece of treat under one cup. Keeping in mind which cup the treat is under, move the cups apart by pushing them away from you on either side as far as you can. Then lift up the cup under which there is *no* treat and put it back down. Release your dog and see which cup he goes to first. Many dogs make what's called the A-not-B error, meaning that they run to the cup you last touched, assuming that is where you want them, even though they know that the treat is under the other cup. Dogs who make this error seem to get over it after a few tries of running to the wrong cup but then finding the treat beneath the other.

Socio-Emotional Development Exercises

Bonding

EXERCISE 1: Play a quick, vigorous game of tug or toy toss three times for approximately twenty-second periods. End each session by saying "Will you Settle?" in a soothing voice and offering your dog a small piece of treat. After a pause of approximately five seconds, resume play.

EXERCISE 2: Find a way to get close to eye level with your dog and gently massage the sides of his face while speaking in a soothing tone for approximately thirty seconds. You can make eye contact with a dog who trusts you, but do not stare, as that can be disconcerting even for a dog who loves you.

EXERCISE 3: Pick up a piece of treat or kibble, making certain your dog sees you. With your hands hidden behind your back, put the kibble in one hand. Then present your loosely closed fists to your dog and ask him, "Which hand?" If he designates (by nudging or pawing) the correct fist, open your hand and let him eat the kibble. If he chooses the wrong fist, open your empty hand briefly and say, "Uh-oh." Present your loosely fisted hands again and repeat, "Which hand?" Repeat four or five times.

EXERCISE 4: Set out twenty pieces of low-value treat and four small pieces of high-value treat. With your dog near eye level, hand feed him pieces of treat one at a time, alternating low-value treats with an occasional high-value one. As you feed, speak softly and calmly to him. Tell him how awesome he is or describe in great detail the most delicious thing you've eaten recently. Say anything, as long as you are speaking with affection.

Trust

Drape a sheet between two chairs, forming a tentlike structure. Position your dog on one side with you on the other. Either by using a leash or by positioning your chairs strategically, make certain that your dog cannot go around the drape to reach you. Then call him through the drape, rewarding with kibble when he makes it through. If your dog is fearful, you can help alleviate his concerns by first crawling through the drape beside him.

Self-Reliance and Competence

EXERCISE 1: Put several small treats in a cardboard box and let your dog sniff his way to the treats. Start with the box top open, but slowly progress to closing it by tucking the flaps so that your dog will have to work to get into the box. You can use multiple boxes with treats in only one to make it harder for your dog to find the treats.

EXERCISE 2: Using two cardboard boxes placed on their sides, create a barrier between you (and the treat in your hand) and your dog. Leave only small, nearly hidden gaps for him to push through. Frequently change the positioning of the gaps (with your dog out of sight) so that he has to determine new ways of getting through the barrier. Playing this game a few times in a room that has two access doors is another great way of helping your dog realize that sometimes there is more than one way to accomplish a task. After checking to be certain door B is open, go out door A and close it behind you. Call your dog. You can repeat that several times and then try exiting through door B and leaving door A open.

EXERCISE 3: Toss a few handfuls of kibble across a patch of grass or pine straw while he isn't looking and then ask your dog to hunt for his supper by giving him a verbal prompt such as "Want to Hunt?" so that he knows he has your blessing to search for and gobble up his kibble. If you do not have a safely fenced-in area where your dog can hunt, keep him on a long, loose leash, making it clear that you will follow his lead. Providing opportunities for your dog to feel successful and capable is tremendously important, and this exercise is all about letting his instincts guide him.

Social Competence

Every dog needs to have ample opportunity to socialize with new people and other dogs. Set up meetings for your dog with many different friendly strangers, both human and canine. Don't be alarmed if your dog growls or snaps at other dogs who violate the Code of Canine Conduct or if other dogs correct your dog for some violation. It's important for dogs to stand up for themselves—I'm glad when I see mine do it, and I'm grateful when other dogs help mine understand the rules of social interaction without actually hurting them. The verbal corrections that a usually friendly dog offers a dog who has violated a rule of conduct can sound scary, but the result is actually beneficial rather than harmful, and neither dog seems to have any negative feelings for long.

Physical Development Exercises

Sensory Awareness

Collect items that feel, sound, or look different from the things your dog typically encounters in daily life, and allow him to play with them one at a time. I like to go to Goodwill to find inexpensive toys that are oddly shaped, crinkle, or make strange noises—anything that expands my dog's sensory perception, helping him to become comfortable in his environment. Go for walks with your dog in areas with unusual surfaces, such as sidewalks with grates or paths that are sandy or rocky.

Gross Motor Skills

Teach your dog to run up and down stairs and then to walk up and down stairs one step at a time. Teach your dog to jump through a Hula-Hoop held first on the ground and then at slowly increasing heights. You may need a helper to hold the hoop at first as you coax your dog through, but eventually you should be able to hold the hoop and ask your dog to jump without coaxing.

Fine Motor Skills

EXERCISE 1: Use an inexpensive rubber ball, such as those sold for children in drugstores. The ball should be light and of appropriate size for your dog to be able to move by nudging with his nose. Hide a piece of kibble or two just underneath the front of the ball and say "Nudge"—a way of asking him to nudge the ball with his nose to discover the kibble. When your dog nudges the ball, say "Yay you!" so he knows that the action was appropriate. Slowly eliminate the pieces of kibble under the ball as your dog begins to recognize that it's fun to nudge the ball even when there is no food underneath.

EXERCISE 2: Teach your dog to bat with his paws by putting a treat or a few pieces of kibble under a cardboard box and saying "Bat," asking him to bat the box over to get the food. Since this exercise is to help your dog know how he can use his paw, you might want to lightly rest your hand on the box so you can keep it from falling if your dog uses his nose rather than his paw. When your dog places his paw on the box, help him tip it over if necessary.

Body Awareness

Make a rocker board by placing a pillow under the center of a half sheet of plywood. You can also find easy directions on building rocker-type boards for your dog online. Encourage your dog to stand on and walk over the rocker board to increase his balance, body awareness, and self-confidence.

Fitness

Dogs, like humans, benefit from slowly building up their physical stamina with aerobic exercise. Walking is safe for most dogs regardless of age, as is swimming, provided your dog feels comfortable in the water and you are always available to supervise. More-strenuous exercise such as jogging and running should be cleared with your dog's veterinarian. Vary your routes and routines if possible to keep things exciting. By the way, your fitness level will likely improve as well.

What Great Teachers Know

Great teachers know that, for students of all species, the most important thing is to give them the desire to succeed and the belief that they are capable of so doing. In order to flourish, students of all species need to be confident that their basic needs—food, water, shelter, and safety—are met. But being prepared to learn involves more than just the basics of survival. We learn best when we approach our studies with a positive outlook about our learning environment, our teachers, and our subject matter.

In *The Happiness Advantage,* positive psychologist Shawn Achor explains, "It turns out that our brains are literally hardwired to perform at their best not when they are negative or even neutral, but when they are positive." In contrast, when our stress levels are unmanageably high, we shut down. As an example, Achor describes how students in higher education who are under the pressure of a pending deadline often turn away from the very thing that could help them succeed—their social network—when their stress levels are unmanageably high. Likewise, dogs can feel stressed while learning new things. It is imperative that we keep the bond with our dogs particularly strong during these times. We can do that by taking frequent play or massage breaks during coaching sessions.

Treat Rather than Reward

There is a clear distinction between external rewards we may offer dogs, such as treats or toys, and the internal rewards they experience when they know they are making us happy. External rewards are merely the flip side of punishment. As such, they are equally controlling. Internal rewards facilitate internal control, while external rewards give control to whoever is providing the reward.

Dogs, like humans, experience a flash of enlightenment when problem solving. This sense of satisfaction when they figure things out causes an internal flood of good feelings. In turn, the positive sensation helps motivate them to perform the behavior again and again. I'm convinced that external rewards diminish, or at least distract from, that internal flush of success, and as a result can actually be counterproductive.

Some people believe that providing external rewards helps facilitate the bond. I disagree. Imagine being a dog for a moment. Someone offers you a piece of delicious food for sitting. What are you focusing most of your attention on—the person asking, the act of sitting, or the yummy piece of food? The food would be your primary focus. Then you may think briefly about sitting as the reason for the food. From a practical standpoint, you might take note of the person who asked you to sit so that you'd remember whom to ask for food in the future. However, it's unlikely to make you like him more.

Continuing to think like a dog, imagine having a handler randomly give you treats *simply for being you*. This is *treating*, as opposed to *rewarding*, and it should happen frequently during instruction, provided the treat isn't offered in concurrence with a specific behavior the dog performs. If we frequently pause in learning sessions and give our dogs treats, the attachment developed will be with the person giving the treats. Rewards, though they may have their place, increase the dog's focus on the reward. Treats are gifts that increase the bond between handler and dog. *Treat your dog for merely being awesome rather than rewarding him for doing as you ask.*

Mossy, a goldendoodle and one of our Canine Assistants dogs, gave me a firsthand look at the power of educating dogs in each of the three domains. She was only four months old when I took her with me on a trip to Miami for a presentation about the work we were doing at Canine Assistants. It was an important meeting with the executives and sales staff of a large potential corporate donor, and I would be speaking in front of nearly a thousand people. While Mossy would not be required to demonstrate her service-dog abilities, I was counting on her extra-adorable puppy factor to help win the audience over to our cause. My experience has proven that puppies are difficult to resist, even for business-oriented, corporate types. Still, flying in a plane and appearing before so many people was a lot to ask cognitively, emotionally, and physically of such a young dog.

She was perfect in the car on the way to the airport. Once we arrived, she confidently rode with me in the elevator from the parking deck to the ground floor. I directed her to a small area of pine straw just before the entrance to the terminal, and she immediately went to the bathroom. All of this was great, but the real challenge would be navigating the Atlanta airport, one of the busiest airports in the world and an exercise in chaos management. It is almost always massively crowded, and while the security checkpoint lines there move fairly quickly, they are often long and populated by impatient people who are running late. So I was nervous as Mossy and I approached security. I had to quickly remove her cape, leash, and collar to avoid a time-consuming by-hand security scan, and then walk her off leash to the scanner by lightly cupping her chin in my hand. Mossy had to wait while I went through the scanner first, and then she followed me on my call. I repeated the whole cupping-the-chin business while waiting for her leash to appear on our side of the conveyor belt. And through all of this, she was perfect.

Next, there was an extraordinarily long line for the elevator, so I decided to try Mossy on the escalator. I decided that if she showed any hesitation, we would go back and wait for the elevator. But she wagged her tail happily as we stepped onto the steep escalator, and continued with the happy tail wagging as we boarded the shuttle to our concourse and, once we got there, as we rode up a second escalator.

Finally, we boarded the aircraft and Mossy settled at my feet easily and fell soundly asleep. Most of our service dogs when they travel seem to at least sit up when the plane takes off and lands, but Mossy felt so relaxed and secure that I had to shake her awake once we'd reached our gate in Miami. I attribute much of Mossy's comfort to the extraordinary bond we share and to the developmental exercises we'd practiced before our trip.

Mossy behaved beautifully once we got to the presentation in Miami, supporting my efforts at our meeting with powerful self-confidence. I was proud to have her with me, and upon our return I made sure to thank all of the Canine Assistants instructors and volunteers who had been instrumental in her early education. In addition to her composure, Mossy was respectful and attentive to me and, most important, totally content. She clearly had deep roots and strong wings, proof that our new Bond-Based Choice Teaching was working.

Seven

Dogs Need Role Models

Have you ever seen a five- or six-year-old light up when they see an older child? It is absolutely adorable and occasionally a little pitiful how much the little ones want to be like the *big kids*. They emulate every move the older children make. We are the big kids in our dogs' eyes. They want to be like us. They want to do what we do. The willingness of our dogs to imitate our actions and synchronize with our demeanor makes them highly motivated learners who are easily taught.

The desire to *fit in* is a survival mechanism in social species, and this desire is a powerful tool in helping our dogs behave in ways we deem appropriate. In most cases, we simply need to become our dogs' role models, showing them what to do. When dogs have a secure attachment to us and feel like part of our group, their desire to fit in will do the rest.

The Canine Assistants Bond-First Teaching Model

I used to believe that the ability to direct a dog's behavior en-hanced the bond between handler and dog, but the Canine

Assistants dogs have taught me that the reverse is actually true—
that it is easier for dogs to bond first and then later learn to follow
direction, if any directions are indeed needed.

Our two-week-long recipient camps at Canine Assistants take
place six times a year. On Monday morning, twelve to fourteen
people walk or roll into our classroom hoping to find the canine
love of their lives. Every day of camp is stressful and chaotic, but
none more so than the first. I still remember when I first introduced the Bond-First teaching model to the staff. I didn't want
the recipients to ask the dogs for behaviors initially, but rather
focus on bonding and let the dogs direct their own behaviors.
The idea had just occurred to me the day before, and I'd been
working on it in my mind until late that night. There simply
hadn't been the opportunity to discuss the new concept with
the staff until the very morning camp was starting. This was the
most significant change that we'd ever made to our camps, and
the staff fell quiet after my short presentation, pondering what
I meant. Finally, someone asked me to explain what it would
look like, practically speaking. "That's a work in progress," I responded.

What we really want, even with working dogs, is for them to
understand what behaviors are appropriate in various contexts.
There are certain behaviors, such as not pulling while on leash,
retrieving dropped objects, and flipping a light switch, that we
have to actually teach our dogs so that they can add them to
their repertoire. But mostly our dogs already know how to do everything we'd like for them to do. The teachable part is helping
them figure out when to use those behaviors.

The inaugural Bond-First recipient camp proceeded with
remarkable smoothness, though we were making changes all the
way through, and sometimes in the middle of exercises. While I
initially intended that we would eliminate names and cues completely from the first week, a total and complete departure from

how camps had always been run, we quickly realized that a recipient would need to use his new dog's name to get his attention. Also, it proved necessary to add back the phrase "Better Hurry!" to signal that it was time for the dogs to relieve themselves. And we decided to leave in the cue word *Wait*, meaning freeze in place, as a safety precaution if the dogs were headed for trouble or dangerous situations. Otherwise, we eliminated all words and physical gestures previously used to direct behavior.

In earlier camps, exercises on that first day had always been stressful, as recipients attempted to cue their new dogs to perform behaviors with little reason behind them for the dogs to understand or accommodate. And if the dogs did not respond appropriately, the recipients felt as if they and their dogs had both failed.

The bond-first premise was so straightforward that I couldn't believe we hadn't tried it before, and the results were amazing. We asked everyone to do bonding exercises with their dogs and otherwise simply leave the dogs to their own devices. It was magical. When the people moved, the dogs moved. When the people stopped, the dogs stopped . . . and usually sat. When the people stayed still for more than a minute or two, the dogs would lie down. The new approach was incredibly empowering and much less stressful for the people and the dogs, allowing genuine bonds between partners to develop at astonishing speed.

It's critical for recipients to bond with their dogs, the sooner the better, the stronger the better. So for the first four days of camp, the Canine Assistants instructors, who have worked for many months with the graduating dogs before the recipients arrived, are rarely present. Early in our history, we discovered that the bond between instructors and the dogs they'd worked with for so long caused new recipients to struggle for their dogs' attention. Feelings were hurt, focus was lost. With the new approach, after spending the better part of the first week with their partners, the dogs barely glanced when their old instructors reappeared. The dogs were self-assured, secure, and clearly in love with their new people. It was stunning to watch.

We know that part of the bond is chemical, but I'm convinced that the release of those positive chemicals was made possible when we turned the system upside down. Recipients were focused on helping their dogs feel secure and connected. The dogs were able to figure out what behaviors were appropriate in given settings without superfluous words or signals blurring the picture.

The bond-first concept proved so successful that we continued using it throughout the entirety of camp rather than just the first few days as originally planned, and this is how we run our camps today. The dogs had already learned what behaviors might be needed—just as your dog will learn from you in your teaching sessions. We simply needed the dogs to want to figure out what to do and when to do it. With these new teams, we focused on bonding, and that connection encouraged the dogs to make choices that were pleasing to their new partners.

Graduation for that camp was as joyful as any in the more-than-twenty-year history of Canine Assistants. In addition, the first two weeks after people returned home with their new dogs, typically a time of great transition, was shockingly, almost disturbingly, trouble-free. Our aftercare coordinator, who normally receives multiple calls the first week after camp, sat by a silent phone. Finally, she was compelled to initiate contact with the recipients, making certain that all was well. It was. This group didn't need us—the recipients and their dogs had their new best friends.

It was easy to encourage the dogs to synchronize with their people. It seems that dogs are hardwired to do so. And they do more than simply *act how we act*. They appear to *feel how we feel* as well.

Dogs Empathize with Us

Dogs, it seems, feel our pain and seek to ease it, which I believe means they have the ability to empathize. Some experts hesitate to credit dogs with true empathy and instead suggest that their actions are the result of a kind of emotional contagion, rather than true understanding of an emotional situation. The subscribers to this theory say that dogs are responding to their own feelings of distress—seeking comfort rather than seeking to comfort their person. But I believe there is evidence to the contrary.

Two psychologists from Goldsmiths' College in London tested empathy in dogs by using a modified version of a procedure that had been successfully used to measure empathy in toddlers. In these tests, a dog's caregiver and a stranger were seated approximately six feet apart. Each person, in turn, would talk, hum in an odd staccato fashion, or pretend to cry.

The setup produced results that make it difficult to deny that dogs experience both empathy (an understanding that others are experiencing distress) and sympathy (a desire to comfort those in distress). Most of the dogs tested responded to the crying of both their caregiver and the stranger by going to that individual and offering comforting gestures, such as licks, nuzzles, and snuggles.

But the dogs responded to the humming with, at most, a look. Clearly, dogs are both empathetic and sympathetic to people.

The communion that's possible between man and dog at times seems incredible, and yet I see it every day at Canine Assistants. Several weeks ago, we received a note from a mom who had attended a recent recipient camp with her son. It was not the first time I'd heard from a reformed skeptic, but it wonderfully describes the magic that can happen when trust is nurtured between man (or boy) and dog. She wrote:

I have to admit that I was skeptical about how Jennifer says a dog picks the person as opposed to the person choosing his dog. I just didn't see how that was possible. But I certainly came to be a believer.

It all started when Jennifer had Oke, a big, white goldendoodle, out of his crate visiting with other recipients. My son, William, was sitting along the back wall minding his own business, not even looking at Oke. But the big dog saw him. He started pulling toward William and wouldn't stop until he reached him. My son began to pet him softly. In an instant, much more than a physical connection was made. It was like electricity was flowing through each of them to the other.

The next day of camp, Oke wanted no part of his kennel. Finally, William was asked to get him out so he would stop barking, and for the rest of the day, Oke rested quietly by the boy's feet. The bond between the two was already remarkably strong.

While we were at the mall for training in public places, William's legs began getting tired. When this happens, he tends to rock side to side in an effort to balance himself. Without any instruction, Oke instinctively knew to put his body against William to help secure him. As I watched Oke support William, I knew that the boy and his dog were now sharing their feelings without words. It seems that they think alike and love each other more than I can describe. This dog has transformed my son's life.

Oke and William are just one example of the deep, powerful connection that is possible between dogs and humans. Nurturing this connection, based in trust, benefits us just as much as it benefits our dogs.

Quit Acting Like Your Father's People

Mothers throughout the Deep South can be heard warning their children against inappropriate behavior with the phrase "Quit acting like your father's people." While such an admonishment would not apply in my own family, as my husband and his people are well above reproach, I love the expression. Try using it sometime. It's quite a handy way of completely denying that unwanted behaviors are, in any way, shape, or form, your responsibility.

Declaring "Quit acting like your father's people" is also a great way of making the tone of your voice convey that whatever your dog is currently doing isn't appropriate. A vital part of our job as our dogs' role model is to help them understand what simply *isn't done*—or shouldn't be done. I don't believe that it's acceptable to allow our dogs to behave poorly in the name of the bond. Appropriate behavior is another necessary survival skill for dogs . . . and people, for that matter. You are looking out for the best interests of your dog, yourself, and those around you when you alert them to the fact that what they are doing isn't okay. Some people will actually be surprised to hear me say this. There are those who believe that being kind and being overly permissive are the same thing. They are not.

My friend recently told me about a woman she knows who gives her eight- and ten-year-old sons a great deal of choice. My friend explained that the two boys like to walk around with their hands down their pants. The mother allows the boys to decide if they'd like to stay home, in which case they may keep their hands down their pants, or go out, in which case they must keep their hands visible. My friend asked me—given my desire to afford dogs all possible choice—what I thought about the mother's approach. My response was swift and strong: "I'd tell those boys to quit acting like their father's people and take their hands out of their pants. I'd also insist they wash them." There are simply some things nice people, or nice dogs, don't do.

Facial Expressions Revealed

In 1872, Charles Darwin published a book titled *The Expression of the Emotions in Man and Animals,* in which he described certain emotions he asserts are universally expressed on the faces of mammals. Though there is discussion about overlapping categories, many modern researchers still believe there is strong evidence for the universal facial expressions of seven emotions: anger, contempt, disgust, fear, joy, sadness, and surprise.

Sometimes I'm convinced that dogs are able to read human expressions far more easily than we've previously imagined. It would make sense, given the difficulty we have in hiding our feelings from them. We know from research that dogs have the ability to read expressions of happiness and disgust. Consequently, deliberately making those facial expressions is a great way to convey information to dogs.

At Canine Assistants, we have begun using a new method of expressing approval or disapproval. We give our dogs an ostensive signal, such as saying their name (always kindly), and then we use facial expressions to express our approval or disapproval. In the past, when we wanted dogs to stay away from something, we would say, "Leave it." I never liked that cue, because it always proved difficult to keep people from shouting it. Today, by combining an ostensive signal and a facial expression, we've been able to change that approach, and we now use the word *Ick* in lieu of *Leave it. Ick* is social information that indicates something is unsafe and best avoided. It is not a command. Social information allows a dog to formulate his own response.

For example:

- Dog begins to sniff at an inappropriate item.
- Handler says dog's name (ostensive signal) so that the dog will make eye contact.
- Once the dog makes eye contact, the handler says "Ick" while wrinkling his/her nose in an expression of disgust.

My dog Jack slicked his ears back and stepped away from the forbidden object the first time I used Ick. Jack and I are very much in sync, and not every dog will learn as quickly, but it's something all dogs can learn eventually. Once your dog understands the more dramatic Ick face, you can begin to minimize the expression and eliminate the verbal Ick altogether. Today, with Jack, I can say his name (ostensive signal) and barely wrinkle my nose, and he recognizes that as direction to *leave it alone*.

Learning by Watching

Until recently, many scientists thought dogs incapable of imitation, which is a form of social learning. In the past, when scientists saw evidence of one dog copying another, they would dismiss it based on a principle of animal psychology known as Morgan's Canon, which states that animal behavior should be explained as simply as possible. For example, if dog A watches dog B open a gate latch, and then A opens the gate latch himself, that may be an act of imitation *or* it could merely be that watching dog B made dog A want to investigate the latch. Undoubtedly, such fundamental problem solving accounts for some learning in dogs, but so does true imitation. Knowing that dogs can imitate the actions of people gives us an amazing opportunity to teach them things in a way that reinforces the bond between us.

From the very beginning of my work at Canine Assistants, it was apparent to me that dogs were learning from other dogs, sometimes outright imitating them. Mirror neurons (discussed in Chapter Two) are a large part of this ability. But *learning* a behavior and *performing* a behavior are two completely different things. To investigate, I conducted an experiment with seven of our six-month-old puppies to see if they would voluntarily perform a behavior they'd picked up by watching another dog.

First, Puppy One was taught to *bow* by encouraging him with a treat to lower his front legs and head as his rear end remained elevated and saying "Bow" to help him add the word to his vocabulary. As Puppy One was learning, his accomplishments were noted with clapping and saying "Yay you!," and the other six puppies were in crates, positioned with an unobstructed view of the proceedings. After about five minutes with Puppy One, I put her in a crate and brought out the other puppies, one at a time.

I asked each, "Can you bow?" I repeated the request several times after intervals of approximately twelve seconds. After exactly two minutes and ten seconds, the puppy presented a slight bow, for which I clapped. Then the puppy began to consistently perform the bow. Puppy Three took only twenty-four seconds to produce a bow, and each subsequent puppy thereafter bowed more quickly than the previous. The lone exception was the fifth puppy tested, who spent two minutes running around the room before bowing, reflecting his slight ADHD. Nonetheless, this method has proven tremendously effective in teaching dogs new behaviors, and we use it regularly at Canine Assistants.

Dogs can also learn from watching people. When Dr. Adam Miklosi came to Canine Assistants to film a PBS documentary on our program in 2010, he enthusiastically described a study that he and his fellow researchers in Budapest were working on, called "Do as I Do." Miklosi explained that the project had started when his colleague Dr. Jozsef Topal began working with a service dog named Philip, using a technique developed in the 1950s for teaching chimpanzees to copy human behaviors. Philip learned to duplicate his handler's actions, and what he demonstrated was amazing. He could and would imitate all manner of behavior, even realizing that he had to use his mouth in place of human hands to perform certain actions.

Based on Topal's work with Philip, Miklosi and other researchers created additional studies that involved a larger group of dogs and investigated numerous components, including whether the dogs would show *deferred* imitation as well as *immediate* imitation. Deferred imitation, a minute or more after demonstration, requires the individual to retain a mental representation of the action, an ability some scientists still believe is beyond the cognitive scope of dogs. But Miklosi's study determined that it isn't. Working with a brilliant trainer named Claudia Fugazza, Miklosi administered a series of tests to eight female dogs of various breeds, designed to determine if the dogs could imitate behaviors after waiting periods, ranging from twenty-four seconds to ten minutes. All eight dogs performed almost flawlessly. Fugazza believes the dogs could have gone even longer, but the researchers limited the time in deference to the handlers.

Imitation in nonhumans is a highly controversial subject, since it requires serious cognitive prowess. One must observe the behavior of another, remember the action using representational images, and then repeat the action, making any adaptations necessary to accommodate physical differences between observer and demonstrator. Example: If a dog observes a human move an object with his hands, the dog must remember that action and determine how to accomplish the same task without opposable thumbs.

While most people consider imitation to be any action learned through observational social learning, many scientists proclaim that *true imitation* requires the learner to repeat a novel action learned and facilitated only by watching a demonstrator perform the same action. If these tight criteria are not met, then the action is not considered evidence of true imitation. There are some less cognitively complex methods, means, and motivations that can account for behaviors that appear to be imitative but technically are not, including the following:

> ENHANCEMENT means the drawing of the observer's attention to a place (known as *local enhancement*) or an object (known as *stimulus enhancement*), thus making it more likely the observer will move toward the location or interact with the object.

> EMULATION occurs when the watcher sees the demonstrator being rewarded for being in a location or interacting with an object and seeks the reward himself.

> DISCRIMINATED FOLLOWING occurs when a demonstrator acts as a lure for another to follow. When rats learn to go through a maze, following the lead rat is not as much evidence of imitation as it is a mere display of following behavior. The others would be as likely to follow a string or a feather as they would the lead rat. This behavior is more follow-the-leader than imitation.

> EMULATION OF AFFORDANCES means making use of what another has shown to be available. If one person, trapped in an elevator with others, reveals the presence of a previously unseen exit by climbing through it, those who follow the demonstrator's example are emulating affordances rather than truly imitating.

> IMPRINTING is the recognition of and affinity for members of one's own species or surrogates thereof, allowing for rapid learning about what it means to be a member of that species. Imprinting occurs soon after birth, when individuals are most open to forming attachments.

Ethologist Konrad Lorenz did research on imprinting in the 1930s that revealed that the newborns in certain species, such as geese, often imprint on the first suitable moving mammal they see. In fact, Dr. Lorenz became a "mother goose" to many greylag hatchlings, which were often seen waddling behind him.

MIMICRY is the copying of physical characteristics. The edible viceroy butterfly is an excellent example of mimicry, taking on the physical characteristics of the inedible monarch butterfly in order to avoid being eaten by predators.

CONTAGION is the replication of behavior in a species. Example: In 1996, scientists began noticing that dolphins in western Australia were holding large conch shells out of the water in order to shake the fish lodged inside into their mouths. A mere handful of dolphins were seen doing the conch shake in 1996, but by the following year the behavior had become widespread. My son describes this as the jumping-on-the-bandwagon effect.

Teaching *Like Me*

At Canine Assistants, we use an adaptive, Bond-Based version of Mikloski's "Do as I Do" to teach our dogs certain behaviors. We call our approach *Like Me*. While Like Me does not strictly meet the scientific definition of imitation, it is a less formal approach to encouraging dogs to replicate what we do. This method has transformed learning in our dogs, enabling them to grasp new behaviors in single sessions rather than the several weeks it used to take.

PREPARATIVE SESSIONS

Choose three behaviors you can demonstrate for your dog that he can easily replicate, such as putting your foot or hand on something, turning in a partial circle, or nudging an object. Make certain these behaviors are simple processes rather than more complex ones requiring multiple steps. For example, dropping an item on the floor may seem like a one-step process, but it actually involves multiple steps: walking to the item, picking up the item, and dropping the item on the floor. Ultimately, your dog will be able to do multiple-step action replications, but it's best to keep things simple in the beginning. We have found that behaviors involving objects rather than simple body movements seem easier for dogs to replicate, but you may choose any single-step behavior you'd like.

LIKE ME SESSIONS

Have your dog off leash in a safely enclosed quiet area, preferably an indoor room containing a chair and whatever items you need for your behaviors.

Warm up with Sit and Stand. Start by calling your dog close and, as he watches, sit in a chair. After you sit, look at him as if you expect him to do something. You can talk to him a little to keep him from walking away, but don't touch him. You may say the words "Sit" and "Stand" if you'd like to add them to your dog's vocabulary. The second his rear end hits the ground, tell him how brilliant he is and hand him a treat (as a distraction) as you stand up. If you use a wheelchair, then move forward a pace or two rather than standing. Wait until he stands (you may need to move a couple of steps at first) or moves forward, then tell him how brilliant he is and, as you feed him the treat, sit back down yourself or stop your forward movement. It is important to get the timing right. This exercise helps your dog synchronize with you.

Your dog must be able to wait long enough to watch you perform the behavior you are asking him to replicate. The dog is more likely to wait if he feels calm, which is why it's important that these exercises be done off leash in a quiet, safely enclosed area. If your dog struggles to watch you without participating, you may have someone else lightly restrain him while you demonstrate.

After the warm-up exercise of Sit and Stand, demonstrate a simple behavior your dog can easily copy, such as jumping up or putting your foot on a chair. The performance of the behavior should not require you or your dog to move more than several steps to complete, so situate any needed objects accordingly. After you perform the behavior, applaud yourself—we clap and say, "Yay me!" Once you have demonstrated the behavior, say, "Can you Like me?"[2] You may look in the direction you'd like your dog to move, point with your finger or gaze, and even move toward the object if necessary. When your dog does the demonstrated behavior, clap for him, and say "Yay you!" If your dog does not do the requested behavior, repeat the demonstration and the request. If your dog still doesn't perform the behavior, try another behavior.

When your dog is routinely able to copy single-step behaviors, you may move to two-step behaviors, and so on, until your dog is copying behaviors requiring even five or six steps. Your dog will tell you how much he can do.

As social animals, dogs want to do the *right* thing in the eyes of others. You will find that it is easy to help your dog understand what the *right* thing is when you serve as his role model.

[2] You can add a word or words describing the action you're asking your dog to copy, such as asking "Can you Jump like me?" if you'd like to use the exercise as a way of teaching new vocabulary.

Eight

Acting as His Advocate

In 1997, British evolutionary anthropologist John Archer wrote a paper in which he suggested that dogs don't really care about people and only behave as if they do because they are manipulative social parasites. While for the past quarter of a century, Archer's view of dogs has sparked heated debate, my work with service dogs, for equally as long, has convinced me that no debate is necessary. Archer was wrong. Dogs have the capacity and the willingness to contribute to our lives in a positive way, and any failure of that to occur is our fault alone. In other words, humans alone determine the value of dogs in human society. And it's to our advantage to value them highly and advocate for them fiercely. As a matter of fact, of all the roles you play in your dog's life, none is more important than that of *advocate*.

Look with Eyes of Love

Dogs view us through a haze of affection, and they deserve the same return gaze. As we seek to advocate for our dogs, let's begin by viewing them with affection.

Here's an example of what I mean:

A few weeks ago, I received two emails on the same day from two friends about their dogs who were having accidents in the house. Though both friends had similar concerns, the emails had vastly different tones. In the first, my friend Sharon wrote, "Life with Fred is awesome but I could use some advice about housebreaking. No matter how often I take him out, he's still finding 'hidden' places to go in the house. How can I help him figure out that his bathroom is outside?" In the second email, my friend Kate wrote, "Jax will not stop pooping in his crate. Help!!!"

Both of my friends love their dogs, but notice that Sharon starts her email on a very positive note and then goes on to ask how she can help Fred. In Kate's email, it is clear that she holds Jax fully responsible for his accidents. Based on my experience, I'd say that Sharon looks at Fred with affection, while Kate doesn't have that same affectionate filter when viewing Jax.

In my estimation, Sharon will have an easier time and a more pleasant experience helping Fred change his behavior than Kate will with Jax. The anger and frustration felt when you allow yourself to believe (erroneously) that your dog is deliberately trying to make your life miserable isn't fair to the dog and does nothing to actually help fix the problem. When you get upset with your dog, take a deep breath and remember that he adores you and whatever he did wasn't done in an effort to hurt or anger you.

My own experience with the eyes of love provides another example:

Fundraising is a constant challenge for us at Canine Assistants, and our CEO, who also happens to be my brother, once had the unfortunate job of calling me and reporting that a large corporate donation we'd been counting on would not be coming in. It would be an understatement to say that I took the news badly. I cried like a two-year-old whose ice cream had fallen off its cone.

As I sat holding the phone and weeping, my dog Jack watched me intently. Before I realized what was happening, he stood up, walked across the room, gently reached up, took the phone with his mouth, and crunched it beyond repair.

I could have been angry and reprimanded Jack for destroying the phone. But instead, I asked myself *why* he had done it, and I was deeply touched when I realized that it had been because of his affection for me. Jack loves me. He saw me crying while holding the phone, and in his mind, the phone was the source of my distress, so he killed it. Problem solved. There are many who'd claim that I'm anthropomorphizing Jack with my explanation, but I strongly disagree.

There is a principle in science known as Ockham's razor that states that, when choosing between hypotheses, it is most appropriate to choose the one that involves the fewest assumptions. In other words, the simplest explanation is the best. I cannot think of any simpler explanation for Jack's behavior, though I'm sure there are those who can. Additionally, I say that my perceptions are my own, and as long as they work to my dog's benefit, that's okay.

Ask Why, Not What

When working with dogs—and children, for that matter—we have a tendency to want a solution even before we understand the problem. For example, we want a child to sit still when we ask, but we may fail to address the important fact that the child's full bladder was the reason for his fidgeting in the first place (something that happened to a young teacher friend of mine with distressing results). If we don't understand the problem, we can't change the behavior in any meaningful way. We must understand *why* it is happening. Once we comprehend the *why* of a situation, the *what* to do about it usually becomes clear. But until this knowledge is gained, you can only hope to suppress the behavior, which in turn often leads to other problems.

When a dog is barking excessively, it is imperative to figure out *why* he is barking. If the dog is bored, then he needs to be given socially acceptable ways of alleviating his boredom. If you merely suppress the barking in some way, which is undoubtedly quite unpleasant for the dog, he may develop other coping behaviors, such as digging or chewing on furniture.

A man and his son, who had Duchenne muscular dystrophy, had been on our waiting list for years. When they finally received the call that a dog was available, father and son traveled hundreds of miles to meet their own personal version of Lassie, the dog they hoped would make all things better. But the father was a very practical person, and our Bond-Based method of teaching had him baffled. He'd anticipated a different approach to directing his son's dog once they were matched—he wanted commands. Since we don't allow recipients to direct their dogs for the first week of camp, this father felt they were being denied the means to succeed.

When we sat down in my office to discuss the situation, his frustration was palpable. And I did understand. Completely. But I also knew that if I handed him a list of words he could use to get his son's dog to perform certain behaviors, I would be seriously limiting the potential of the relationship between the child and his dog.

"What do I say if the dog is pulling on the leash and I need to stop him?" he asked.

"Why?" I said.

"Because he might pull my son over and hurt him," he said, his growing frustration apparent.

"No, I'm sorry," I replied. "I wasn't clear. If the dog is pulling on the leash, rather than giving him a signal to make him stop, you must ask yourself why he is doing it in the first place." I gave him a moment to think about it before I suggested some possible scenarios. "It might be that he hasn't gotten enough exercise and just can't contain his enthusiasm—which you can solve by letting him run around a bit before attaching him to your son's wheelchair. Or he might feel like he is walking alone because he isn't getting enough attention. Or maybe he just has gotten into a bad habit—in which case all your son needs to do is talk to him and give him a few treats as they move. But if I give you a word to make the dog stop pulling, you will use it. That might fix the problem temporarily, but it won't address the reason it's happening in the first place. It would be like putting a Band-Aid on an infected cut. It would make things seem okay when they aren't."

Luckily, that explanation resonated with both father and son. There is always a reason behind your dog's actions. It is critical that we do all we can to figure out the why behind the behavior if we hope to fairly and effectively change it.

Give Him Control
(Unless He's Acting Like His Father's People)

I see so many problems caused by people not allowing their dogs to exercise any measure of control in their own lives. Lack of control can be frightening, seriously undermining a dog's self-confidence. Self-confidence grows from feeling capable of making good choices—meaning your dog must be given the opportunity to self-direct. Lack of control, and therefore lack of self-confidence, often results in behaviors that we find undesirable, such as barking at other dogs when on leash.

You can help your dog develop a feeling of control by giving him time to assess risk for himself. When he is faced with a frightening object, allow him to escape to a safe distance. Then allow him to determine when, or if, he wants to approach that thing he finds scary. Simply knowing that he has some choice in the matter increases his self-confidence and reduces his fear dramatically.

Two of our adolescent puppies were recently having trouble with this very behavior—barking at other dogs while on leash. It wasn't happening when they were at the Canine Assistants farm, but it occurred when their volunteers took the young puppies home and walked them through their neighborhoods. Barking when on leash, though a common fear- or rage-driven behavior, is highly stressful for the human handler. It's embarrassing to have a dog others perceive as out of control or aggressive. Our service dogs are held to a very high standard of behavior, and this barking was a situation that had to be addressed immediately.

As I've mentioned, when a dog exhibits problematic behaviors, our first and only question should be *why*. Why is the dog displaying this behavior? If we don't understand the *why*, then any attempt to alter the behavior is likely to be a temporary fix at best, addressing the immediate symptom while leaving the root cause untreated. As long as the core issue goes untouched, problems created by it will recur and persist.

In this case, we had to first ask what type of *bark* the puppies were making. Was it merely an attempt to instigate play with the other dogs they saw, or was it a fear-based, don't-come-any-closer-until-I-better-understand-you bark? Using a dictionary of dog sounds (which appears in this book as Appendix E), the volunteers decided it was fear-based in both puppies. So, *why* were they afraid?

Age appeared to be a factor, since both Canine Assistants puppies developed the behavior at approximately the same age. A secondary fear period (the first being at around eight weeks of age) can occur in dogs during adolescence, from approximately six to ten months. This is the age when a dog's level of awareness changes. Suddenly, the young dog is looking at the world through the eyes of an adult, but without the coping mechanisms that experience will later bring him. In addition, hormonal changes may play a part in periods of adolescent fear unless the puppies have been spayed or neutered at a young age.

In addition to age, there may be a genetic component to this behavior. A similar behavior was observed in the puppies' father, Butch. Though he had never been reactive toward other dogs while on leash, he did not like having other male dogs in his yard, and he tried frantically to breed with any female visitors. Butch was a stud dog, so his response seemed fairly typical for an intact male. Still, for these puppies, there was something more going on. Perhaps it was an indication that Butch, who was exceedingly aware of other dogs, had passed this characteristic down to his progeny. Dogs who are highly focused on other dogs are more likely to perceive their behaviors as threatening.

So while it was likely that these puppies were at an age and had a genetic propensity for vocalizing toward other dogs, we nevertheless needed to understand what specifically was triggering their response. The sight of other dogs was their *on-alert* prompt. My guess was that being on leash was acting as the response trigger, given that they'd displayed the behavior only while leashed.

Walking directly toward another dog is an enormous violation of the canine code of conduct. But humans don't usually know this and often walk dogs directly toward one another. Once this faux pas has been committed, it becomes difficult for the dogs to determine who's at fault, leading to questions about adherence to the code and whether surrounding dogs are dangerous.

In addition, being *leashed* is being *restrained*, and *restraint* can potentially prompt the rage system. Imagine for a moment that you are in your dog's shoes. Someone is walking toward you in what you fear might be a threatening manner while you are tied by rope to your dear, but oblivious, foreign-speaking friend. What would you do?

First, I'd look at my friend in an attempt to gain insight into the situation. If her attention was not on me, I might begin vocalizing my concerns. Likely my friend would then begin yelling in her foreign language while pulling tighter on the rope. I'd have no way to understand her language, so my obvious assumption would be that she too was alarmed about the approaching stranger. At this point, my rage system would likely activate and I'd go nuts.

It would not enter my mind that my friend was, in fact, upset with my behavior. After all, I was alerting her to a potential danger, right? I'd believe she had tightened the rope between us because she was afraid. Since she clearly would be of no help, it would be up to me, and me alone, to frighten away the stranger. The rope would make it impossible for me to flee and freezing wouldn't help, so fighting would be the only option available. In the future, it would be easy to see why my anxiety levels would rise with each similar encounter. My barking would become more likely and intense, especially if it had kept strangers from attacking in the past.

This was a reasonable explanation for our puppies' behavior. And while we understood why it was happening, we still needed them to stop. So rather than merely addressing the behavior, we needed to address the root causes, fear and rage. We didn't want to simply say, *This barking at other dogs is unacceptable and needs to stop* — even if we taught the puppies a different, more acceptable behavior, such as turning their heads — because the true problem wasn't what they were doing but rather *why* they were doing it. It was the feelings we needed to help them conquer.

In order to truly eliminate the fear, we'd have to think about its root cause. When being walked on leash, the puppies were afraid other dogs might hurt them. They felt, rightfully so, that they were without the ability to control the situation. The solution was to *give them control*. We needed to allow the dogs to dictate their desired response.

As mentioned, time and distance are the keys to giving dogs control. They need time to decide the appropriate course of action for themselves, at a distance from which they feel comfortable.

Keeping these elements in mind, here's how we handled our barking puppies:

First, we got a twelve-foot-long leash. We don't recommend retractable leashes because, if dropped, a retractable leash can continually hit the back of a dog's legs, spooking the animal. We prefer a plain leash, folded loosely in the hand.

Second, we found a calm, predictable dog-and-pet-parent team to act as our helpers, stationing them approximately two hundred yards away. We asked them to begin walking slowly toward us. When the puppies (taken one at a time) noticed the helper dog, we dropped the slack in our leash in an effort to determine each dog's preferred course of action. Most dogs will go backward, seeking to put more distance between themselves and the approaching dog. However, some will go toward the oncoming dog in an intimidating manner to make the other dog retreat.

If the dog preferred to put more distance between himself and the approacher, then that's what we allowed. If, in that process, it became apparent that the approaching dog was stressing our dog, we led him away at a 90-degree angle before he could start barking. I prefer walking away at an angle rather than turning all the way around, which eliminates a dog's ability to keep track of the approaching dog. We worked at this twice a day, practicing our walk three or four times each session. With each trial, we observed the puppies allowing the other dog to get incrementally closer without showing distress. We watched their body language carefully so that we could lead them away prior to their vocalizing.

If we found that either dog wanted to chase the approaching one, then we had the person walking the other dog turn at a 90-degree angle and walk away. We continued working twice a day. And, of course, we continued monitoring stress levels, so that we could signal the other dog to turn before the puppies had a chance to pull forward or vocalize. Gradually, we saw the puppies begin to allow our helper dog to get closer, finally passing by without reaction.

Remember, giving your dog a sense of control, the ability to make his own choices, is critical for his well-being. You can help him develop this feeling of control by giving him time to assess risk for himself. When he is faced with a frightening object, allow him to *escape* to a safe distance. Then allow him to determine when, or if, he wants to approach that thing he finds scary. Simply knowing that he has some choice in the matter increases his self-confidence and reduces his fear dramatically.

Advocating Good Behavior the Bond-Based Choice-Teaching Way

WHAT NOT TO DO

First, let's talk about what not to do. Do not attempt to control your dog's behavior using cues and directives. One of the primary goals of the Bond-Based approach is to help your dog learn to control his own behavior—not to do it for him. Therefore, cues and commands are largely counterproductive. But even without cues, we must understand that cooperation is *voluntary*; otherwise, it's called compulsion.

If you read my second book, *In a Dog's Heart*, you may remember that I typically like the large dog-food companies. They're the ones that have the ability to do comprehensive testing on their products, making them the safest you can feed your dog. I've taken a good deal of criticism from those who believe small boutique foods are superior, and I understand their point of view. Still, I continue to believe that the larger companies make good food and genuinely care about the well-being of dogs. So you can imagine my dismay upon reading the following recommendation on one large dog-food company's website:

> . . . But sometimes he WILL make a mistake, and he
> needs to learn what's right and what's wrong. So if you
> cannot prevent the error, you will need to discipline him
> appropriatcly.

So if you fail to keep your dog from making a mistake (because you haven't taught him properly or set him up to succeed), you should discipline and correct him? This is not the least bit fair or even reasonable.

The site went on to list recommendations from professional dog trainers on how to use environmental corrections to control your dog's problem behavior, including sprinkling the bathroom garbage with hot pepper to cure a dog of the nasty habit of rummaging through the trash, and using a noisy pile of tumbling cans to deter a dog from stealing food off the kitchen table. These methods were actually described as "a great way to instill dog discipline, as long as he doesn't become skittish because of the technique."

The site at least went on to acknowledge that some submissive dogs might be frightened by the "powerful medicine" of setups, and advised that in those cases the dog's owner should contact a professional trainer for help in devising the right plan for the dog. But why even recommend these painful, fear-based methods in the first place? Why do people believe that it is acceptable to frighten a dog so that he will not continue to do something so benign as digging through trash or stealing food from the table? The dog does not think he is doing anything wrong. Remember the Canine Code of Conduct? Under the laws of dogdom, he isn't. In addition, a dog who digs in the trash and shreds available paper is probably doing so to self-soothe when left alone. In which case, causing him further anxiety seems particularly cruel.

In both of the above scenarios, the solution to these behaviors is simple. Place the bathroom trash out of reach, leave the dog something else with which to occupy his time, and don't leave food on the table. Take responsibility. Remember, dogs are in many ways comparable to young children. It's like the case of a two-year-old child touching a hot stove: If dogs cannot understand why they shouldn't do something, the onus is on you to prevent the behavior.

Another section of the website's write-up discusses the use of choke and pinch collars, but cautions that they should be used with care in order to avoid choking or other physical damage. The site provides further examples of ways to discipline a dog, such as alpha rolls, scruff shakes, shaker cans, and squirt guns, and claims that "many dogs need physical correction at some point in their lives."

Unfortunately, this kind of misguided advice is not uncommon. Too many in the dog world still cling to outdated, counterproductive, inhumane techniques, but these methods harm us all. As a species, most of us understand the importance of fairness and cooperation. Our entire civilization is built on these codes of behavior. In our professional and personal lives, we know that we should behave fairly and we expect others to do the same. We simply need to remember that the nonhuman members of our social groups deserve the same consideration.

PREVENTING PROBLEM BEHAVIORS

The first step in preventing unwanted behaviors is always to try to get to the bottom of what is causing them in the first place.

FOOD STEALING

For behaviors like counter surfing and food stealing, the underlying cause can be as simple as the desire to eat accessible food. So addressing the underlying cause of the behavior in this situation is as simple as making the food inaccessible to the dog. Problem solved. Puppies are unlikely to grow up to be adult dogs who hunt for available food in every environment if they don't learn as puppies that such hunts can have positive results, so please *do not* leave food available for stealing.

JUMPING

As we've discussed, since dogs are social animals they often try to lower their anxiety levels by seeking to increase their feelings of social support. This can translate into a need to make physical contact with the people in their immediate environment, including such behaviors as jumping up on them. If you are at the other end of a dog's leash, it is *your responsibility* to provide enough social support to keep his paws on the ground. If your dog jumps on you, it means he's not getting enough social support and you need to go *Two Hands, All In* with him by rubbing softly under his ears, telling him what a good boy he is, and slowly leaning forward so that he ends up with four paws on the floor. Keep massaging and talking until he relaxes enough to keep all four paws on the ground. You will quickly learn to recognize when he is relaxed enough for you to stop massaging.

When someone else approaches your dog, you must be the one to go *Two Hands, All In* until you are certain that your dog is relaxed enough not to need to jump on the new person. Remember, you are always responsible for making certain your dog can behave appropriately in any given situation. Bad manners are never okay. However, behaviors such as jumping are symptoms of a core issue, and rather than using traditional approaches that treat the symptoms only, we must look further for the why and seek to eliminate the causes of unwanted behavior.

MOUTHING THE LEASH

A number of dogs, especially young dogs, seem to enjoy holding their leashes in their mouths when being walked. This is a favorite trick of the dogs at Canine Assistants and one that we discouraged for many years. Until, that is, I realized, contrary to what most professionals say, this is not a behavior we should try to stop. "Reciprocal walking" with their human partner makes dogs feel far more secure than does simply being led. As social animals, connectedness is key, and what better way to feel connected than a leash held by both person and dog. This connection has proven to be so valuable for our partnership that I designed the *We Leash*®, which attaches to the dogs' harness or collar but also has an extension that attaches to a toy, designed to be carried by the dog himself.

Traditional training has told us we should discourage our dogs when they try to increase the connection between us by doing things such as holding the leash in their mouths. This is the very opposite of what we should do. We must actually encourage our dogs' secure attachment to us in whatever form it takes.

Advocate Kindness

We know that moral behavior is essential to the survival of social animals, and no creature is more deserving of fair treatment than our dogs, who often seem to care more about us than they care about themselves. There are two primary areas in which our present treatment of dogs could use some work: what we ask of them and how we ask it.

"What do you see when you look at this photo?" I asked my son.

"I see a dog who looks absolutely miserable."

Crud. That was my impression as well, but I was hoping that I was being overly sensitive. The photo was of a precious little boy who looked to be seven or eight years old, lying next to a gorgeous black female Lab. The child was grinning in delight. In stark contrast, the dog, head-halter strap across her nose, looked pathetic. It wasn't a look of fear as much as it was one of utter resignation. The dog looked hopeless.

Obviously, there is no way to know how she truly felt, but she certainly seemed unhappy. It would have saddened me to see this photo under any circumstance, but it was the picture's placement that was truly distressing. It was the photo for the lead story on an international working-dog association's website. The Lab was the little boy's service dog.

Since dogs are so willing to cooperate with humans, it's especially important that we are careful not to take advantage of them. I would love to be able to say that all assistance dogs work because they enjoy it, but I cannot. When a dog is trained using fear or force, he is likely to end up too afraid to refuse to work even if he hates what he's doing. Likewise, a dog in a choke, pinch, or shock collar, or even in a head halter, which many consider humane, has exceedingly little freedom of expression or ability to exercise control over his personal situation.

Some time ago, I watched a three-year-old girl on a national TV news program with her service dog who'd been trained to carry an oxygen tank that assisted the child's breathing. The dog was wearing a pinch collar, undoubtedly to give the child the ability to control a dog who outweighed her by a significant amount. As the child was being interviewed, her small hands jerked repeatedly on the leash. I'm absolutely certain that she did not intend to be unkind to her dog—there's no way that this three-year-old could have known she was doing anything wrong—but pinch-collar spikes hurt when a leash gets tugged. Worse still, in a photo that was shown of the child and the dog in the broadcast, the young goldendoodle was clearly wearing a shock collar.

I can understand how this happened. The girl's parents wanted a service dog who could make life easier for their precious child—placing service dogs with people who need help is what I do for a living, and it can be a wonderful thing. But it troubled me deeply to see how harshly the dog was being treated. He could just as easily have been taught and handled with kindness. If he wasn't willing or able to follow the directives of the child, then a parent or other adult could have helped. A three-year-old shouldn't be without adult supervision anyway.

I'm sure that many people probably worried about the dog after seeing that segment, but few felt comfortable commenting. It seems harsh to say anything negative about such a cute child and such caring parents in so difficult a circumstance. But the truth is that with a shift in perception that is as simple and intuitive as what I'm suggesting in this book, the situation could be so much better for both dog and person.

I discussed my concerns regarding forcing dogs to work for people using compulsion, such as shock or pinch collars, with Steve Dale, a radio show host and writer of a syndicated column for the *Chicago Tribune*. Steve is a wonderful man and a kind, dedicated animal lover. He wrote a column about our discussion and my beliefs, and as you might imagine, the response was swift and harsh. Some people called me an "animal rights freak." Others claimed I was a hypocrite for continuing to work in the service-dog field given my concerns. One person called me "dirt," perhaps meant as a compliment, as in nourishing, life-sustaining soil. Not likely. I think he simply meant the plain, stick-to-your-boots-and-require-vacuuming kind of dirt.

Certainly, the unpleasantness had an effect on me. I am, after all, my mother's child, ever anxious to see people happy— especially with me. But often people read what they want to read in a newspaper article. Steve had expressed my desire to see working dogs treated with the utmost respect, though some may have inferred I was advocating that assistance dogs be done away with completely. This is not the case at all. In fact, I think well-treated working dogs are the luckiest animals on the planet. After all, they get to spend all day with the person they love most in the world. My hope is simply that more people will focus on the *well-treated* part. And unfortunately, as I see it, much of the service-dog industry is still not doing that.

Since the vast majority of working-dog schools use punishment in training their dogs, I was excited to hear about a guide-dog school where clicker training was being used, not my preferred method, but far better than force and intimidation. My disappointment was nearly overwhelming when, several months later, I learned the program was combining their use of clickers with physical correction. By using the clicker, you are asking the dog to voluntarily offer behaviors, to cooperate with you. To combine a request for collaboration with punishment is horrifying and counterproductive. This sort of treatment isn't necessary, and it certainly isn't fair. The handling of working dogs should be exemplary, setting the highest standard for pet parents rather than providing dreadful examples of what the science informs us *not* to do.

I have come to understand that those who train using aversives are simply interested in what dogs can do *for* mankind, not in what dogs can do *with* mankind. We must replace our need to dominate with a willingness to collaborate. We must advocate, not just for our dog, but for all dogs.

Daisy is a border collie puppy I encountered in a rescue facility, where she was both under extreme stress herself and causing severe anxiety for those people around her. She was fearful when people approached her food or toys, and she snapped, snarled, and generally screamed *Get away* in the only way she knew how. Daisy looked and sounded scary, but she hadn't bitten anyone. And I don't think she will, provided no one tries to handle her fear through aggression. She has been evaluated by three different trainers, myself included. One trainer recommended euthanasia immediately. One recommended that the staff at the rescue organization "toughen up and show her who is boss." I don't agree with either conclusion. She is literally fighting for her life, and if people won't cooperate with her, it is a fight she will lose.

It would be a shame to put this dog to sleep. When I evaluated her, I found that 99 percent of the time, she was as sweet and loving as you could possibly ask. She clearly expressed her need for personal space, understandable for a dog who had been mistreated and abandoned. In addition, she was extremely teachable. It took only a few sessions to get her comfortable with trading with me for any item in her possession. Daisy was clearly willing to cooperate. Showing Daisy "who is boss" using aggressive techniques, such as leash corrections, pinning her to the ground, or kicking her behind the ribs (all techniques recommended by the "toughen up" trainer), would be a formula for total disaster. This little girl just needs a safe foster home where she can learn that some people can be trusted. You will be happy to know I've found her a good temporary home . . . in my living room.

The Four-Paw Test

Over the years, Canine Assistants has received wonderful support from Rotary Clubs, and, in fact, I've been asked to speak at a number of their meetings. I've always been impressed with many elements of the organization, but the singular part of Rotary that has had the most effect on me is their Four-Way Test.

THE FOUR-WAY TEST

Of the things we think, say, or do:

- Is it the **truth**?
- Is it **fair** to all concerned?
- Will it build **goodwill** and **better friendships**?
- Will it be **beneficial** to all concerned?

Translated into over a hundred different languages, this guide for living is recited by Rotarians at every meeting and acts as a foundation for their personal and professional relationships.

This is such a great focusing principle that I propose a similar guide for our relationships with dogs.

THE FOUR-PAW TEST

In all dealings with dogs:

- Is it **fair** to all involved?
- Is it **kind** to all involved?
- Does it help build a **trusting relationship** between dog and caregiver?
- Is it **beneficial** for dog and caregiver?

When we can answer *yes* to these questions in every facet of our dealing with dogs, from breeding to teaching to handling to husbandry, we will finally be good advocates for our dogs, as *fair to* and *caring of* them as they are of us.

Nine

The Gift of a Dog's Love

The hum of a new text message made me stop what I was doing and look down at my phone. The message was from a dear friend. It said simply, "How do you survive this?"

She had just lost her eight-year-old dog to cancer, so I knew what she was asking. Before I could respond, she sent another text. "Sorry to bother you but I don't know how to get through this," she continued. "I cannot imagine even a single day without my Luke. I got up this morning, made it to the kitchen, saw his still-full bowl of food, and ended up in a heap on the floor, sobbing. Everything in this house seems to make me think of him. I'm falling apart. Dog commercials hurt; Facebook posts of dogs hurt; walking past his kennel hurts. I can't stand it."

Ugh . . . I understood her feelings all too well. "One hour at a time" was the best I could offer. I went on to suggest that there would come a time when she'd realize that Luke loved her far too much to ever truly leave her, and she'd begin to feel his presence—in her other dog, in her husband, and even in herself. And I believe this. The one card that helped me most when my mother died was a single line: "For no one loved is ever lost and she was loved so much." And I believe the same is true for the animals in our lives.

People who haven't truly loved an animal might think it crazy to grieve so passionately when a dog dies, but those of us who have get it. And while my friend hasn't yet reached this point, there will be a day when she understands that it was because she loved Luke so joyously in life that she grieved with such desperation when he died. Love that strong deepens your capacity for joy even as it leaves you more vulnerable to its loss. It is a trade-off that many of us have sworn in moments of grief that we'd never make again, and yet we usually do. Time proves that love is more powerful than pain.

It seems almost surreal that we can have such an intense connection to another species—that many of our strongest relationships are with animals who don't share our perception of the world, our moral code, or even much of our language. What is it that makes us love dogs so much that we'd literally risk our lives for them? They aren't strictly necessary for our survival. Most cost us far more money than they produce. So what is it that makes them invaluable in our lives? Perhaps our differences are part of the reason we can connect so deeply. Maybe not being able to measure yourself against someone makes him easier to love. Or possibly, it's his vulnerability . . . or ours. But I think the most likely reason of all is that our dogs love us unconditionally. When we return that love, we benefit every bit as much as they do.

Two summers ago, a handsome young man sat on the floor in the classroom at Canine Assistants, his back to the wall, his eyes blank and hollow. For the first two days of recipient camp, he remained motionless. He was a Special Forces veteran suffering from PTSD. He had lived through unspeakable horrors and now seemed isolated and detached. I felt an overwhelming debt to this man and really wanted to help him, but I was afraid we wouldn't be able to reach him.

Matching him with the right dog was difficult. We had wonderful dogs available, but none who found a bond with the soldier. I was struggling. In desperation, I thought of Ginny, a particularly kind and intuitive young female doodle, not designated to be in this camp.

Their meeting is seared into my brain. The young dog took one look at the man and sailed across the room into his open arms. Ginny whined as she nuzzled him like he was her long-lost love. She picked him and, by doing so, she changed him. He no longer sat against the wall. The haunted expression he'd worn was replaced in an instant with a smile of sheer, unadulterated joy. In the end, I was right about not being able to reach him myself, and thankfully I was right about Ginny's gift.

Scientists have long known that stress and other negative emotions can shunt us into a sort of survival mode where our actions and behaviors become limited to the familiar, for as long as a threat exists. These familiar responses are known as our *specific action tendencies*, and Dr. Barbara Fredrickson, a psychologist and leader in the field of positive psychology from the University of North Carolina at Chapel Hill, has developed a hypothesis about how we build up our pool of specific action tendencies, called the Broaden-and-Build Theory.

Dr. Fredrickson suggests that positive emotions and experiences broaden our awareness and encourage us to be more curious about the world around us and to try new things. These new thoughts and behaviors, experienced during good times, eventually become part of our overall repertoire and are available to us even under times of stress. The larger our pool of responses, the more likely we are to survive and flourish in times of stress and anxiety.

Further studies indicate that those who enjoy positive emotional support and have a broader range of these action tendencies are healthier than those without such relationships. This is as true for our human-animal relationships as it is for our human-human ones. So it would hardly be a stretch to conclude that having a positive relationship with our dogs will lead us to happier, healthier, and more fulfilling lives.

Dr. Fredrickson and her collaborators published an intriguing paper in 2013 in *Psychological Science* that opens with this sentence: "People who experience warm positive emotions live longer and healthier lives." And the paper goes on to present abundant evidence supporting this assertion. For some time now, researchers have understood that having positive relationships with others is as vital for our physical and mental health as maintaining a healthy weight and being a nonsmoker. And in turn, there is evidence that those with better health have an easier time experiencing positive emotions. Dogs, by giving us positive social relationships, can actually help us live longer.

A Mutual Responsibility

Though I first told this story in my book *Through a Dog's Eyes*, it is worthy of repetition.

When Ben was fourteen years old, he was in an automobile accident. While he survived, the injury to his spinal cord was severe and permanent, and required him to use a ventilator in order to breathe. To make matters worse, Ben's mother was at fault for the accident, and he was her only child.

Ben wanted desperately to regain some semblance of independence, but his mother's overwhelming guilt about the accident and fear of losing him made that difficult. Ben's ventilator would occasionally become clogged with secretions and shut down, triggering an alarm, and someone would have to flip a switch to suction and reset the system.

When Ben was sixteen years old, he became a Canine Assistants recipient. We'd agreed to teach a dog to *Go get Mom* when the alarm bell sounded, in addition to the other service-dog skills, such as picking up dropped objects, opening doors, and turning lights on and off. The dog was a small female golden retriever named Roxie.

Roxie adored Ben from the very beginning of their relationship. I was apprehensive about Roxie learning to respond to the alarm, so we relentlessly practiced during camp. And it worked. For the first few months they were together, when the alarm sounded, Roxie executed the plan flawlessly, quickly alerting the mom. Then one day something went wrong.

Ben's mother had gone for the mail, something that usually took her under a minute, but this time a neighbor stopped her at the end of the driveway. As bad fortune would have it, this was the moment Ben's ventilator shut down.

When Ben's mother returned to the house, she found blood covering the foyer. Before she could figure out what had happened, Roxie grabbed her sleeve, pulling her into Ben's room. Though Ben had briefly lost consciousness, he was regaining his awareness as she reached him. His ventilator was functioning normally, but Ben explained that it had shut down. Before he lost consciousness, he saw Roxie go behind his chair toward the vent switch.

Clearly Roxie, who they now realized was bleeding from both front paws, had flipped the switch. There could be no other explanation. She had been taught at Canine Assistants to use her nose to flip light switches, and she had seen Ben's mom reset the vent toggle. It was not out of the realm of possibility that Roxie figured out how to do it herself.

The real mystery was the source of the blood. Ben and his mom rushed Roxie to the vet, who explained that Roxie had clawed something so hard it had ground her front nails to the quick, the sensitive tissue above the hard part of the nail.

One look at the family's heavy wooden front doors, bloody and gouged, told the rest of the story.

Not only did Roxie display an astonishing amount of intelligence and composure in flipping the ventilator switch, she showed even greater heart in her efforts to alert Ben's mother. As anyone who has accidentally clipped the quick when trimming a dog's nails can attest, it hurts badly. Roxie hurt herself to save the child she loved, something she would willingly have done again and again if necessary.

As this story makes abundantly clear, our dogs feel a responsibility to protect us—it's instinctual. And given how attuned our dogs are to us, we, in turn, have a responsibility to them.

Dr. Greg Berns, a neuroscientist at Emory University, leads a team who are performing fMRIs on dogs in an effort to examine how the canine brain responds to various stimuli. Dr. Berns has discovered that there is a striking similarity between dogs and humans in both the structure and function of the caudate nucleus, a key brain region that sits between the brain stem and the cortex and is filled with dopamine receptors. Dopamine is a neurotransmitter linked to motivation and reward, and caudal activity on fMRIs, as measured by increased blood flow, is indicative of a pleasurable response to stimuli.

In an op-ed piece in *The New York Times* on October 5, 2013, Dr. Berns reported: "In dogs, we found that activity in the caudate increased in response to hand signals indicating food. The caudate also activated to the smells of familiar humans. And in preliminary tests, it activated to the return of an owner who had momentarily stepped out of view."

Simply stated, we seem to make our dogs happy. This is reassuring news to those of us whose caudate radiates brightly upon seeing our dogs. But at the same time, it is also compelling evidence of our dogs' emotional complexity, and our enormous responsibility toward them. As Dr. Berns continued in his op-ed piece: "The ability to experience positive emotions, like love and attachment, would mean that dogs have a level of sentience comparable to that of a human child. And this ability suggests a rethinking of how we treat dogs."

When I was a teenager suffering the agony of young love gone bad, my mother taught me an important lesson: that only I could determine my worth. I could decide I was worth a penny or a trillion dollars. She went on to explain that the value I placed on myself would determine the way other people treated me for the rest of my life. Our dogs don't have the opportunity to declare their own worth. They need us to do it for them. Let's do that, shall we? Let's declare them priceless and treat them accordingly.

Conclusion

More Than We Ever Imagined Possible

A little girl, no older than four and wearing a dainty pink dress, stood pressed against the chain-link fence, intently watching a group of dogs playing. She seemed to have wandered away from her mother, who was struggling to wrangle two other young children. At one point, the dogs ran past the little girl, chasing a tennis ball, and she took off running after them along the fence line. Suddenly, she tripped on a tree limb, falling hard and scraping her chin. She began to cry.

One of the dogs in the playgroup, a young, sleek Vizsla, heard the child's sobs and came running. The dog looked at the weeping child and then dashed away. In a few seconds, he returned, holding the much-prized tennis ball. The other dogs were in frantic pursuit, but the Vizsla wasn't about to surrender the ball. He looked at the child again and tried to press the tennis ball through a gap in the wire fence. It didn't fit. Undeterred, the dog began frantically digging in the dirt below the fence, all the while deftly protecting the tennis ball from his playmates. Finally, he'd dug a hole large enough to accommodate the ball and nosed it through to the young girl. She ceased crying immediately and in seconds was laughing loudly. The dog then proceeded to gather every toy he could find in the park, pushing each one through the fence to the child, enlarging the dirt hole as necessary.

The girl's mother and siblings finally appeared and I approached them. "Your dog certainly loves you a whole, whole lot," I said to the little girl. The mother quickly explained, "Oh, that isn't our dog . . . we don't have a dog. We just stopped to watch while her brother is at baseball practice." As it turned out, the Vizsla belonged to a young man who'd been on his cell phone, at first oblivious to his dog's heroic efforts. When he realized what had happened, he smiled with pride and love shining in his eyes and reached through the fence to give his friend a scratch on the chest.

As I saw it, the dog had been distressed by the child's sobs, and in an effort to alleviate her sadness, he'd delivered the most prized possession available at the park, the tennis ball. No commands, no leash and collar, no clicker, and no food rewards were necessary to make him behave this way. I believe the dog's concern and cleverness were a by-product of what was clearly a great relationship with his human. Feeling securely loved by his person made this dog a better canine citizen than any obedience class ever could. This is just what I have seen time and time again in my work with dogs, and what I want most to help people understand.

Judy Luther and I recently finished teaching our fifth seminar on Bond-Based Choice Teaching, and we were both pleased with the way things went. One attendee had told us when she arrived that she'd heard some people in the dog community saying there wasn't enough evidence yet to prove that Bond-Based Choice Teaching was effective. After the opening presentation, she said she realized that argument really wasn't applicable. She said,

"It's not a matter of Bond-Based Choice Teaching working or not working, because it's a way of *thinking,* not a way of *doing.*"

Of course, she was absolutely correct. It's not a methodology but rather a philosophy. It's a way of thinking that opens up a world of possibilities. The following story clearly illustrates the depth of the potential:

At Canine Assistants, we call the way we work with our dogs "Non-Training at Its Best." We caution our clients that it is likely that one day someone will make a negative comment about the fact that our dogs don't robotically obey commands given by strangers—something many people seem to believe they should do. One of our recent recipients, Eddie, just had firsthand experience with this phenomenon.

He and his service dog, Bee, were in a store when a clerk approached the team, looked at Bee, and told her, "Sit." Bee remained standing. The woman then told Eddie his dog didn't seem very well trained. Without missing a beat, this wonderful young man said, "God bless you, ma'am, for noticing. Bee isn't trained at all, but she is brilliantly educated." Eddie then pulled out a photo of a cup he keeps in the pack on the back of his wheelchair and asked Bee, "Would you please?" Bee pulled a cup out of the pack and dropped it in her dad's lap. Then Eddie asked, "What goes in the cup?" Bee responded by pulling out a bottle of water from the pack and giving it to Eddie. As the clerk watched in stunned silence, Eddie finished the interaction by asking Bee if she was ready to leave, then extending his left hand as he said "Yes" and his right as he said "No." When Bee nosed his left hand decisively, Eddie wished the woman a good day and rolled away.

We have been so busy all these years telling our dogs what to do that we've neglected to ask them what they are capable of doing. In the presence of unconditional love, the answer seems to be *More than you ever imagined possible.*

Why We Breed

For the first six years of our existence at Canine Assistants, we trained only dogs we adopted from shelters and rescue groups. I loved being able to do this. It felt heroic, and we resolutely defended the practice. But not all agreed. I recall meeting a woman who was a service-dog user who insisted that adopted dogs were totally unpredictable and prone to cancer, and that it was unfair to our recipients to use anything less than the best possible bloodstock. I took what she said personally. In fact, I was furious. My beloved dog Nicholas, who slept quietly under the table during our meeting, had been adopted from a shelter. I believed that what the woman was saying was nonsense. It was clear: I was right. She was wrong. After the meeting, I quickly put the unpleasantness out of my mind and we continued adopting.

Almost everyone else seemed quite supportive of our adoption policy. It made perfect sense—save dogs from shelters and use them to help people. It seemed clear that it was a win for the dogs and a win for the people. So I was utterly stunned when I met with the director of the Atlanta Humane Society, a presumed ally, and he told me in no uncertain terms that I was wrong. I wasn't actually helping anything, he said, because I was rescuing only the dogs from shelters who were otherwise totally adoptable. Ugh! I was incensed. I had another naysayer to prove wrong.

The problem turned out to be that he *wasn't* wrong. I was. One day, I found myself racing to a local shelter, having heard that a young Lab had just been turned in. I arrived simultaneously with a representative from an Atlanta rescue organization wanting to adopt the same Lab. She said in a pleading voice that her rescue group could adopt this dog to any one of fifty families on their waiting list and the chosen family would make a donation in return. It was the way they were able to raise the money to look after the dogs who were not as easily placed. It was clear that the dogs we wanted at Canine Assistants, young Labs and goldens, were in highest demand by families looking to adopt. I wouldn't be saving this dog's life. He would be going to a good home regardless. That day I started to rethink my opposition to breeding our own dogs.

The final push toward a breeding program for Canine Assistants came when I realized that what we were asking of these adopted dogs was often more than they could handle. Dogs in shelters or with rescue organizations are all, to one degree or another, traumatized. They've all had a rough go. After adopting, I had to ask them to be brave enough to walk sedately through the Atlanta airport, calm enough to accept being touched by countless strangers, smart enough to learn new behaviors, and kind enough to use those behaviors in service to a human being. Worst of all, I had to put them through another rehoming. Looking at the process from the dogs' perspective made me realize that the kindest thing I could do was let go of my own need to be a hero—a difficult thing to do.

I'm not totally opposed to the idea of using adopted dogs as assistance dogs. In fact, some of the best dogs we've ever had at

Canine Assistants were adopted from shelters or rescue organizations. But service-dog programs have to be extremely careful to select dogs who are mentally and physically healthy enough to enjoy working for a living. Anything else is not fair to the dog or to the recipient who is matched with him. In the case of Canine Assistants, we still occasionally adopt, but only because our breeding program allows us to be cautious and careful with our selections.

Before Canine Assistants started our breeding program, my husband and I looked closely at the protocol utilized by other assistance-dog organizations who have breeding programs. We were stunned and alarmed by the extremely low percentage of puppies, some 25 to 40 percent, who actually graduate. I was barely tolerating the idea that we weren't going to rescue our dogs. The thought that we'd be creating more puppies who might need homes didn't work for me. We had to determine a way to increase those percentages.

We've done pretty well. Over 95 percent of the puppies we breed graduate successfully from our program. In part, that is due to our flexibility in terms of placement. If a dog doesn't love retrieving but has a fantastic nose, we place him as a seizure-response or other medical-alert dog. My husband has also contributed greatly to our high success rate. He discovered a way to nearly eliminate hip dysplasia in our dogs.

Hip dysplasia is caused when the ligament attaching the head of the femur (thighbone) to the hip socket is loose, permitting the femur to rub against the bony part of the socket. Dr. Kyle Matthews, a veterinary surgeon at North Carolina State University College of Veterinary Medicine, realized that preventing growth at the bottom of the pelvis while allowing growth at the top creates an outward arc that better secures the head of the femur inside the hip socket. This prevents the bone-on-bone rubbing that causes the arthritic changes that lead to hip dysplasia. In conjunction with my husband, Dr. Matthews has used our puppies in his research, creating a procedure called juvenile pubic symphysiodesis, JPS for short.

Our puppies have a series of radiographs, known as PennHip, once they reach the age of sixteen weeks, the earliest time allowed under the PennHip protocol. The radiographs make it possible to determine the degree of laxity in the ligament that attaches the head of the femur to hip socket. If a puppy has a ligament that allows the head of the femur to pull halfway out of socket or more, he has the JPS procedure done immediately. Timing is important, since the best results are obtained when surgery is done before twenty-two weeks of age. In addition to doing JPS on puppies who have loose ligaments, Kent also uses PennHip radiographs to select our breeders. Our breeder selection process has significantly reduced the number of puppies who need JPS. This is impressive for an organization that uses Labs and goldens, two breeds known for hip issues.

Additionally, I attribute our impressive graduation rate to the way we raise and teach our dogs. Most assistance-dog programs send their puppies into volunteer puppy-raiser homes when they are approximately eight weeks of age. These incredibly kind people care for the puppy for eighteen months, at which time the dog returns to the program's kennel to complete his training. It's the job of the puppy raisers to teach basic obedience, good house manners, and social skills. It's a difficult job, physically, financially, and, most of all, emotionally. Personally, I cannot conceive of having a puppy until he's a young adult and then simply letting him go — even though I, of all people, understand the significant impact these dogs have on the lives of those who truly need them. Honestly, I'm not sure I could be a puppy raiser, and I'm in awe of the people who can.

At Canine Assistants, we decided not to use puppy raisers, though it's much more expensive to keep the puppies on the farm. We simply couldn't ask others to do what I didn't think I could do myself. In retrospect, it's one of the smartest decisions we've ever made.

Initially, we worried about the emotional health of the families who had to let go of the dogs, but we forgot to worry about the *dogs* themselves. It wasn't until several years into our breeding program that the trauma such a separation must cause the dogs occurred to me. The puppies grow up in a family home, with a warm bed and constant attention, and then suddenly get shipped off to a kennel. It must seem like prison to the dogs. When you consider that many assistance-dog programs still train using aversive tools, such as choke chains, pinch collars, and even shock collars, there is a significant risk of creating confused and unhappy dogs. At Canine Assistants, we prove that there is a kinder, better way.

Thoughts About Breeding Standards

The genetic health of purebred dogs is an exceedingly controversial topic. And no matter what I say, I will likely offend some people, potentially ones for whom I care a great deal. That said, dogs need these issues addressed so that focus can be placed on solutions. Small genetic pools, mandatory under the American Kennel Club (AKC) guidelines, are simply not as healthy as large genetic pools.

Every breed began as a relatively large genetic pool, since every breed started as a mix. Take the golden retriever as an example. The golden retriever is reported as having been developed in Scotland by Lord Tweedmouth in the 1800s by crossbreeding various spaniels, the Newfoundland, and the Irish setter. Tweedmouth wanted a spirited water retriever who was also gentle and kind. He nailed it. However, today's goldens have a wide range of genetic problems, brought on by the strict requirements of "keeping the breed pure." Conscientious breeders are working diligently to eliminate those genetic issues from their dogs, but the limited gene pool does not make it easy.

Golden breeders are fortunate that the standard for physical appearance in goldens, as written by the AKC, doesn't preclude good health. However, it does in some breeds, such as the bulldog. Here are a few excerpts from the AKC standard for the bulldog, dealing specifically with the head, face, and nose:

> **SKULL:** The skull should be very large, and in circumference, in front of the ears, should measure at least the height of the dog at the shoulders.
>
> **FACE AND MUZZLE:** The face, measured from the front of the cheekbone to the tip of the nose, should be extremely short, the muzzle being very short, broad, turned upward, and very deep from the corner of the eye to the corner of the mouth.
>
> **NOSE:** The nose should be large, broad, and black, its tip set back deeply between the eyes. The distance from bottom of stop, between the eyes, to the tip of nose should be as short as possible and not exceed the length from the tip of nose to the edge of underlip. (http://www.akc .org/breeds/bulldog/breed_standard.cfm)

Breeds with large heads and pushed-in faces are known as *brachycephalic*, meaning short (*brachy*) headed (*cephalic*). Without a doubt, they're cute dogs, whose big, baby-like eyes compel us to adore them. But their physical appearance wreaks havoc on their physical function. The huge heads of puppies often cannot fit through the birth canal, precluding a natural delivery. These brachycephalic breeds can also have serious breathing problems. Their nostrils are extremely narrow, leading to potential laryngeal collapse. And while their lower jaws are normal in size, their upper jaws are quite compressed; consequently, their soft palates do not fit properly, resulting in the snorting and snoring so commonplace in dogs such as bulldogs. In fact, when bulldogs bark or pant excessively, their throats can swell, causing life-threatening problems.

In other breeds, the standard of appearance may allow them healthy physical structures but mandate cosmetic changes that do not seem to be in the dogs' best interest. Example: Below are the AKC's standards for the tail and ears of the Doberman pinscher:

> TAIL docked at approximately second joint, appears to be a continuation of the spine, and is carried only slightly above the horizontal when the dog is alert.
>
> EARS normally cropped and carried erect. (http://www .akc.org/breeds/doberman_pinscher/breed_standard .cfm)

There are serious problems with this standard of appearance. Nature gave the Doberman a long tail; consequently, breeders must have puppies' tails *docked* (cut off) when they are a few days of age. Some argue that tail docking isn't painful to puppies. I disagree. When I was a teenager, I worked in a veterinary clinic. On my second day, I was asked to hold a litter of eight puppies while their tails were docked. The puppies were not sedated and the area was not numbed. Each puppy had his tail cut off by a pair of sterilized toenail clippers in between the second and third tail vertebra, still standard procedure for many veterinarians. The puppies screamed. As the vet finished the final puppy, I vomited into the pail that was holding the severed tails. Then I quit my job.

The process of docking tails appeared in history for several reasons. The ancient Romans believed that severing part of a dog's tail or tongue would prevent rabies. It does not. In later times, when it was believed that a long tail assisted dogs while hunting, and hunting was reserved for the aristocracy, those dogs belonging to *commoners* had their tails docked to prevent their use. More recently, certain working breeds have had their tails docked in an effort to prevent injury. However, studies indicate that between 500 and 2,500 tails would need to be docked to prevent one injury.[1]

Ear cropping, done in puppies between six and twelve weeks of age, seems to have started purely for the sake of appearance, though some insist that it improves hearing and helps prevent ear infections, a claim not supported by any data. Ear pain is so miserable that I cannot imagine subjecting anyone to it on purpose. Even worse, several studies have determined that painful procedures experienced by the developing nervous system during infancy, such as the ear and tail cropping done on neonatal puppies, can actually cause problems with pain perception later in life.[2]

A few simple changes to the American Kennel Club's standards of appearance would make a significant difference in the welfare of purebred dogs. Indeed, the United States is one of the few countries considered "first world" where ear cropping and tail docking for cosmetic reasons isn't against the law.

[1] P. G. Darke, M. V. Thrusfield, and C. G. Aitken, "Association Between Tail Injuries and Docking in Dogs," *Veterinary Record* 116, no. 15 (1985): 409; G. Diesel, D. Pfeiffer, S. Crispin, et al., "Risk Factors for Tail Injuries in Dogs in Great Britain," *Veterinary Record* 166, no. 26 (2010): 812–17.
[2] J. L. LaPrairie and A. Z. Murphy, "Long-Term Impact of Neonatal Injury in Male and Female Rats: Sex Differences, Mechanisms and Clinical Implications," *Frontiers in Neuroendocrinology* 31, no. 2 (2010): 193–202; D. Vega-Avelaira, R. McKelvy, G. Hathway, et al., "The Emergence of Adolescent Onset Pain Hypersensitivity Following Neonatal Nerve Injury," *Molecular Pain* 8 (2012): 30. Accessible online at: http://www.molecularpain.com/content/8/1/30.

The Canine Assistants Nursery

Labor and Delivery

- The average gestation period for mama dogs (also known as bitches) is sixty-three days.
- Four to five days prior to their delivery date, bitches are dropped off in the Canine Assistants vet clinic, where their behavior is closely monitored and their temperature is taken every eight hours.
- An X-ray is taken when the mama dog enters the clinic, so that the vet can try to estimate the number of puppies. This is done by counting heads or spinal cords in the X-ray.
- A drop in body temperature (which coincides with a drop in progesterone) is the first sign of labor:

    Normal body temperature range is 101°F–102°F.

    During late pregnancy, body temperature is usually 100°F.

When delivery is imminent, body temperature usually drops to between 96°F and 98.5°F.

- Delivery is expected within twenty-four hours of a temperature drop.
- Over 87 percent of mamas will whelp (deliver) within a three-day period centered on their due date.

Puppy Development Facts

- The ideal weight for golden and Lab newborns is between fourteen and eighteen ounces.
- All pups should double their weight in ten to fourteen days.
- It is normal for them to lose a little weight within the first few days.
- Weight loss, after the first few days, is often the first sign of illness in puppies.
- Newborn weights are checked twice daily for the first week, then once daily until seven weeks of age.
- Puppies are able to smell at birth; this is how they find Mom and then Mom's milk.
- Their ear canals open at approximately fourteen days, and the puppies begin to hear you at about twenty-one days.
- Eyes open at approximately ten to fourteen days, but puppies' vision continues to develop until seven weeks of age.
- Puppies begin using front legs at about six to ten days and back legs at about eleven to fifteen days.
- Initially, newborns are completely dependent on the environmental temperature for warmth. During the first four weeks of life, they increasingly develop the ability to regulate their own body temperature.

Normal Temperature for Puppies:

Week 1: 96°F–97°F

Week 2: 97°F–98°F

Week 3: 98°F–100°F

Week 4: 100°F–101°F

- We keep the whelping room/nursery at a comfortable temperature as long as Mom is present. Pups are easily overheated despite the fact that they cannot regulate their own temperature initially. Only when pups are orphaned is their environmental temperature increased to 85°F–90°F, with 50–60 percent humidity.
- At about three weeks of age, the pups start getting their teeth and the nursery volunteers will start offering them soft puppy food. When the puppies are approximately five weeks of age, mamas will move back home with their breeder families. Puppies remain in the nursery until seven weeks of age, at which time they receive their first set of shots and move to the puppy kennel building. Puppies will remain with their littermates until they are at least sixteen weeks of age.

Raising Canines

The Canine Assistants Socialization and Habituation Protocol

These are the recommended exposures for puppies between the ages of five to sixteen weeks. (Some say the socialization period ends at twelve weeks, but I think for certain breeds, such as golden retrievers, it goes on a bit longer.)

- Children of as many ages, ethnicities, and activity levels as possible
- Men of as many sizes, shapes, ages, and ethnicities as possible. Be sure to include some with facial hair, deep voices, hats on, etc.
- Women of as many sizes, shapes, ages, and ethnicities as possible
- People using wheelchairs, walkers, canes, and crutches
- People in uniform
- People riding bicycles

- People wearing raincoats, heavy coats, using umbrellas, etc.
- People clapping and whistling
- People shouting
- People knocking on the door and ringing the doorbell
- As many vehicles as possible, including cars, trucks, tractors, buses, and golf carts
- Garage door openers
- Elevators
- Escalators (in arms)
- Stairs of all types
- Toilets
- Hairdryers
- Washers/dryers
- Vacuums
- Televisions
- Mirrors of various types
- Footings of as many types as possible, including carpet, slick floors, sidewalks, and grates
- Nail trimming and grinding
- Brushing
- Tooth-brushing
- Helium balloons
- Busy streets
- Crowded parking lots
- Parks (Keep your pup in your arms since he isn't fully immunized.)
- Playgrounds (Keep your pup in your arms, since he isn't fully immunized.)
- As many other animal species as possible
- Bathtubs and shower stalls

Canine Massage Techniques

My friend Melony Phillips, an excellent dog trainer, taught me the most important rule of canine massage: Allow your dog the freedom to move away from you if he so chooses. Massage should be a *voluntary experience* for your dog. You can find a video of Melony demonstrating techniques on one of Victoria Stilwell's eHow Pets posts on YouTube.

Massage your dog only when *you* are relaxed. Any tension you're feeling will transfer immediately to your dog, significantly reducing the benefits of massage. Massages can be as short or long as you and your dog choose. And as a rule, *light touch* is stimulating and *deep touch* is calming.

Techniques

HANDS ON means resting your hands fairly heavily on a particular area of the dog. This establishes a feeling of calm connectedness and is an excellent precursor to a massage. Your hands can be flat on top of the dog or cupping an area from underneath, but be careful not to dig your fingertips into the dog. This technique is excellent for dogs who are very sensitive or who have pain in a particular spot.

SCRATCHING is another nice precursor to a massage. In addition to reducing an itch, scratching can also increase blood flow to the areas touched.

EFFLEURAGE is a long, smooth, gliding stroke that is generally used to begin and end a massage. Your hand should be relatively flat so that all parts are touching the dog, not merely your palm or fingertips. Follow the contour of the dog with long, fluid strokes. Effleurage warms the tissues by increasing blood flow, thus preparing the dog for deeper strokes.

PETRISSAGE is a kneading stroke that lifts, rolls, twists, and gently squeezes soft tissue. It is safest to use light to medium pressure with petrissage. It can be done anywhere skin is loose or there is some bulk between skin and bone, rather than on spots such as legs, where there is little between skin and bone.

COMPRESSION is a pumping action that pushes tissue inward against the underlying bone. This movement can help with muscle spasms. Slow compression is relaxing and can be used on smaller muscle groups. Rapid compressions are more exciting and best used on larger muscle groups.

T-TOUCH CIRCLES, a technique developed by Linda Wellington Jones, are done by picturing a clock on your dog that is one-half to one inch in diameter. Place your fingers on the visualized clock with your middle finger on six o'clock, your thumb approximately two to three inches away from forefinger, and with the heel of your hand resting on your dog. Push in using your chosen pressure (described below) and circle your fingers all the way around the face of your imaginary clock, past six o'clock and on to eight o'clock. You are making a circle and moving a quarter at a time to complete the motion.

T-Touch rates the pressure of massages from *one* to *nine*, with *six* being the maximum generally used on dogs. You can feel the pressure of a *one* by placing your thumb on your cheek and your middle finger on your eyelid and circle with a very light touch. A *three* can be felt by repeating the thumb-on-cheek, middle-figure-on-eyelid test, but this time press more firmly but not enough to feel as if you are squishing your lid against your eye. Repeat that pressure on your forearm. A *six* is simply twice as firm as a *three* and can be tested on your forearm as well.

T-Touch circles can be done anywhere on your dog's body, including on the gums. Adjust the size of your circles and the number of fingers used to the location you are working. It is strongly encouraged that you maintain contact somewhere on your dog's body with your other hand as you are doing your circles and moving your working hand into new positions. The "off" hand acts as a ground connection, a constant attachment point between you and your dog.

Dictionary of Dog Sounds

Dogs make a variety of noises—barks, whimpers, growls—and they all mean something a little different. I've created the following list of dog sounds in part from my own experiences with dogs, but much of it is also adapted from Stanley Coren and Sarah Hodgson's table in *Understanding Your Dog for Dummies* (Hoboken, NJ: John Wiley and Sons, 2011).

Long string of barks with pauses in between each bark = *Hello? Anyone there?*

Quick yips followed by a longer howl = *I want my mommy!*

Bark-howl = *Anybody out there? I'm lonely.*

Howl = *I'm over here.*

Several quick strings of barks with pauses in between each = *Alert—Something interesting is happening.*

String of quick, rapid barks with no pauses = *More Serious Alert—Something immediate is happening.*

Rapid lower-pitched barking without pause = *WARNING—Intruder/Danger.*

One or two mid- to high-pitched barks = *Hi!*

Single high-pitched bark = *Huh?*

Single sharp low- to mid-range-pitched bark = *STOP!*

Single mid- to high-pitched bark = *Do it!*

Bark rising in pitch = *Let's go!*

Stuttering bark = *Playtime!*

Deep, chesty bark = BACK OFF!

Deep growly bark = *Do NOT push me.*

High-pitched growly bark = *I'm so scared.*

Growl with pitch rising and falling = *I'm so scared that I might have to bite you—or run away.*

Baying = *Fall in / We are close to our target!*

Whining rising in pitch at the end = *I really need something.*

Whining with no change in pitch or lower pitch at end = *Let's GO!*

Whimpering = *I'm afraid* or *I hurt.*

Yodeling/moaning/howling in breathy manner = *I am so excited!*

Yelp = *OUCH!*

Series of yelps or screaming = *HELP! I'm dying here!*

Panting = Excitement or stress.

Sighing = *I'm content.*

Acknowledgments

My name alone appears on the cover of this book, but behind every word contained within stands an amazing army of people and animals:

Judy Luther, whose wisdom, commitment, and courage inspires me every minute of every day.

My husband, Kent, and son, Chase, who share with me their brilliant brains and loving hearts.

My sisters Lisa, Katherine, Shannon, and all the Arnolds, Aldridges, Gaines, and Bruners, whose love makes me brave.

My adored assistant, Miranda, and my wonderful nephew, Dudley, who keep me sane.

Wilton and Martha Looney and David and Debbie Scott, whose support is unwavering.

Janelle McBride, whose research skills and amazing instinct make me a better writer and a better educator.

My precious friends Darlene, Vaughn, Kelly, Candy, and Allison, who prop me up time and time again.

The staff, board, volunteers, recipients, and animals of Canine Assistants, who make work a privilege.

To my animal companions, who make life a pleasure.

Victoria Stilwell, Allison Woosley, Abigail Wittenhauer, Susan Howard, Deb and Bill Hatherly, Deb Selinger, Susan Dansbury, Laura O'Kane, Lesley Adams, Brenda Dew, Melody Phillips, Joyce Hagan, and all the attendees of Teach the Teacher, whose talent and dedication fill me with hope.

My agent, David Vigliano, whose tender encouragement and ferocious representation make me refine "possible."

"My Julie" Grau, of Spiegel and Grau, warrior goddess and publisher extraordinaire, who believes with all her heart.

My editor, Jessica Sindler, whose kindness and wisdom have made her a treasured ally and a cherished friend.

Everyone at Penguin Random House, most especially Sally Marvin and Lindsey Kennedy in publicity, art director Greg Mollica, and Laura Van Der Veer and Kelly Chian in production.

And finally, to my brother, Gee, who makes it all possible.

To each of you I give my adoration and appreciation.

And to the readers of this book, thank you for your time and your interest. I wish for you and your dog(s) the best life and love have to offer.

About the Author

JENNIFER ARNOLD is the founder of Canine Assistants, a service-dog school based in Milton, Georgia, and the creator of the Bond-Based Approach® to interspecies relationships. She is also the *New York Times* bestselling author of *Through a Dog's Eyes*, which was the subject of a PBS documentary, and *In a Dog's Heart*. Arnold lives in Milton, Georgia, with her husband, veterinarian Kent Bruner, son, Chase, four dogs, two cats, and a myriad of other animals.

About Canine Assistants

CANINE ASSISTANTS is a nonprofit organization dedicated to the education of service dogs and the people with whom they work such that they may enhance the lives of one another. Canine Assistants does not charge for the service it provides; rather, it relies on the generosity of those who recognize that helping one benefits us all.

canineassistants.org